New African
Literature and
the Arts

MUKIIBI
Owl Forms (front view), terra-cotta, 2¼ x 1¾ feet

New African Literature and the Arts VOLUME 2

Edited by Joseph Okpaku

Thomas Y. Crowell Company
NEW YORK, ESTABLISHED 1834
IN ASSOCIATION WITH THE THIRD PRESS

To Mom and Dad
LOVE

to Laura and Linda and Kat and Sheila

*to Walter Haluk, Prof. Eleanor Prosser and
Stanford University*
FOR A CREATIVE UNIVERSITY EXPERIENCE

*and to Marion Cambel, C. Clement Stone,
the Lloyds, the Grenbergs and the Andersons,
and the many others in Evanston and Rockford*
FOR MAKING THIS EXPERIENCE POSSIBLE.

IN MEMORY OF GRANDMA,
Madame Usekpimi Ogunje
WHOSE LIFE WAS ALWAYS THE SOURCE OF ALL
MY CREATIVITY.
THE THOUGHT OF HER NOW STILL INVARIABLY LEADS ME
TO PUT PEN TO PAPER.

Acknowledgments

I would like to express gratitude to all those who helped make the *Journal of the New African Literature and the Arts* a reality, who devoted much time to working on it or consulting for it with no remuneration other than the joy of seeing every issue of the *Journal* through to its appearance in print.

The family of the *Journal* has consisted of Professors Gwendolyn Carter, St. Claire Drake, Peter Duignan, Joseph Greenberg, G. Wesley Johnson, Gerald Moore, Kwabena Nketia, Roy Sieber, and Obi Wali, all of whom acted as editorial consultants to the *Journal;* Professors Ezekiel Mphahlele, John Povey, Paulette Trout, who have acted as assistant editors for literature; Mary Asmundson, Donald Dodson, Romanus Egudu, Glee Harrah, Dennis Hayes, Kirk Jeffrey, Margaret J. Peters, Karen Fung, Jean Patitucci, Michael Okpaku, Charlene and Trevor Brown, Lynda Esposito, Andrea Hines, Leonard Kibera, Gretchen Van Kleef, Sandra Richards, and Susan Sawyer, all of whom, as editorial assistants, were responsible for every aspect of the operation of the *Journal,* from editorial development to distribution. My special thanks to Ola Oyelaran, Zamba Liberty, Walter

Haluk, and St. Claire Drake, who helped launch the *Journal;* to Julie Taylor, who as special assistant to the editor kept the *Journal* going.

Finally, I owe everything to Laura Davidson and Mary Lynch. As assistant editors, first Laura and then Mary were as responsible for the *Journal* as I have been.

My thanks to everyone and to that curious family called Stanford University. Now that the Stanford days are over and the *Journal* has moved on to New York, it is with great fondness and longing that I recall all those hours of sitting on the arms of chairs in a little apartment editing manuscripts or of stretching on the floor addressing envelopes and fulfilling subscriptions. Wherever they are, the *Journal* will always be theirs, and we will always strive to keep the dream they helped build.

Contents

PROFILES of AFRICAN ARTISTS

Editor's Preface

With the substantial reception of Volume 1 of this series, very little need be said by way of prefatory remarks about Volume 2. This volume reflects a further development of the critical and literary experimentations of Volume 1 and the detailed analyses in several areas of African humanities.

Books like these two volumes, which discuss the composite areas of the arts rather than separate literature from music, from dance, from drama, and from fine arts, are rare. This, however, is the way the arts should be discussed, as the knowledge of one is heightened by the knowledge of the other; and it takes the sum total of all of them to constitute the study of any given culture. One review seemed, in my judgment, to have confused this total approach to the arts with what it called "unevenness." But it has always been my belief that a full understanding of, for example, fiction requires a good knowledge of the critical scholarship on the same fiction. This is true of the other arts.

This was the approach in Volume 1 and I am very pleased that many have liked it very much. I can only hope that Volume 2 will meet with the same reception.

Joseph Okpaku
New York
December 1, 1970

ESSAYS

The Writer in Politics— Christopher Okigbo, Wole Soyinka and the Nigerian Crisis[1]

A BRIEF CONTEMPLATION OF A PASSING DREAM

by JOSEPH OKPAKU

The creative artist has always been a controversial figure in the politics of nations. Together with the intellectual and the scholar, he has generally been regarded as a threat to the establishment. One need not go to ancient Greece for examples—no further than contemporary Greece. Soviet Russia is replete with contemporary examples, the adventures of Stalin's daughter, Svetlana Alliluyeva, being perhaps the most colorful of the lot. All these, however, are instances of literary, intellectual conflict with political practice in societies that have essentially, whether in the Western or the Eastern bloc or somewhere lost in between, acquired a certain stability, or, perhaps, a certain stagnant equilibrium—societies with political systems that operate fairly independently of the people.

1 This essay was written at the beginning of the Nigerian civil war. The war has since ended and Mr. Soyinka has been released and is back as head of the Department of Drama at the University of Ibadan.

In Africa, however, and in a good deal of the so-called "Third World," the situation is different. Following the disruption, by forces popularly described as "colonial-imperialist interests," of the political fabric which in its functional stability and its established mode and order was comparable to the present situation in much of the so-called "Western world," there followed an imposed superstructure. This superstructure owed its stability not so much to its intrinsic validity, which is questionable, but to the essential fact of its being externally imposed and kept in effective operation by the strength of political and military as well as economic power and authority. The result of this, besides its obvious politico-economic consequences, was the termination, for an extended period, of the process of natural growth of political theory, thought, and practice which would normally develop from the basic essences of the societies involved. Consequently, upon attainment of independence (for whatever it was worth) and the partial removal of the politically undesirable and socially unworkable external system, there was created, not a vacuum (as we are often led to believe) but an already budding entanglement of conflicting political preferences. This entanglement was heightened and made more complex by the disastrously one-sided upbringing of many of the so-called leaders of public thought in the theories of Western politics without the necessary emphasis on the all-too-important fact that these theories do not owe their validity to the intrinsic worth, but rather to their coming into being as a natural process of development from the socio-economic and political lives of the societies in which they developed.

Consequently, group after group in the African nations debated whether to abide by the theoretical principles of Western democracy as supposedly practised in the "free world" or to turn to the allegedly more suitable socialist

[4]

philosophy of the Soviet bloc. The African society, we were told, was by nature socialist, presumably (and falsely) in the Marxist sense of the word. The major question, and what did not seem to have made itself obvious to the minds of the politicians and intellectuals alike, was the simple fact that neither of these philosophies was valid for all human society or relevant to the conduct of human behavior in the African society. The choice therefore was irrelevant and, with that, all the international intrigue that has arisen from it.

With the trials and tribulations inherent in the painful return to natural, relevant, and authentic political behavior, there arose in Africa a growing awareness of the contradictions and absurdities existent in the alien practices of the political status quo. Following not unduly on the heels of this awareness was the introit of the social phenomenon all too freely described as military takeovers without regard for the obvious operating forces which are definitely not thanks to the militiamen. As usual, there came into being an overwhelming preponderance of inevitably meaningless literature offering, or rather imposing, simplistic interpretations of the allegedly peculiar political situation. Once again much credit was given to the European powers for delaying, at least for a while, the inevitable bloodshed and barbarism that was doomed to take place if the African were left alone to cope with his political, social, and surprisingly not moral situation.

This was essentially the state of affairs a few years ago as one wandered through the bookstores in New York, Paris, or London, in Abidjan, Lagos, or Dar es Salaam, and saw the titles of book after book explaining the peculiar idiosyncrasies of the African and the brilliant insight of the Western scholar into the African mind; each book claiming to have found the secret of comprehending the tumultuous confusion of the disillusioning African scene. For several reasons, not the least of which was the apparent realization that hardly any one of those books was written either by an African or from a valid African point of view, one reluctantly shook one's head and sighed and dreamed (in perhaps a peculiarly African romantic way) of the years of wasted effort and sadly not inevitable strife and torment that seemed to loom ahead just slightly over the horizon of the seemingly rather late African dawn. One immediately saw, either by reason, or as Léopold Senghor would prefer, by the sensations of the African intuition, that great and sheer energy and effort were being dumped into preparing for and carrying out a journey, the proposed destination of which had not as yet been carefully determined. "Africa," said the World, "has a long way to go." So Africa got ready, packed her old kit bag, and dashed off helter-skelter along this undefined path. What many never stopped to ask was, "Where are we going?" As I said, at the International P.E.N. Congress in Abidjan, Ivory Coast, in August 1967, if where we are told Africa has to go is the present position of Western society, it will be extremely difficult to understand why Africa would even want to bother to make the journey at all, since it is rather obvious, certainly to westerners, that the present state of their society does not seem sufficiently admirable to be worth all the effort Africa would have to make to get there. Why, for example, should Africa spend all her energies sweating hard to diminish the essence of man in his society to the point at which he ceases to be more than a punch hole on a computer card—a mere statistic?

With the admittedly unwholesome sprouting of this irritating questioning upon the general intellectual mood of the still virgin mind of the generation of Africans following upon that which was involved in the actual political struggle (and therefore more blinded and narrowed in vision by its experiences), there arose a conflict of goal, perspective, and purpose. This conflict was inevitably

[6]

bound to grow in complexity and magnitude and, shall we say, doomed to create a gulf between the generation of the political pragmatists, the deeply entrenched elder statesmen now in their fifties and sixties (and some already doomed to die if not dead) and that of the theoretical, intellectual, philosophical, young "sophisticates" who, no less in their naiveté than in their idealism, had a new vision of the Africa for which every one of them felt an almost sensual passion of ownership and belonging. This vision was independent of any other existent European societies or their extensions across the seas. It was a vision with a commitment born of some of the most intense, involved, and intimate calculations that could come only from a group of young people, each of whom planned for Africa the way a parent plans for its child.

It has often been said that this generation of young African intellectuals has been schooled mainly abroad in the citadels of thought and judgment in Europe and America, by which I suppose they mean the universities and societies of these two continents. By implication, it has been maintained that the idealism that these young men hold, and which is claimed to exist in those citadels whence it is supposed to have been acquired, owes itself to the firsthand knowledge and acquaintance with the working principles and ramifications of democracy or Soviet socialism in the everyday life of the communities and nations where these Africans have gone to school. As often happens with a scholarship that aims at proving itself right rather than finding out what actually is, this interpretation is completely bereft of any authenticity in fact. A brief chat with any of these students, whether in Moscow, in Rome, or in Washington, D.C., will reveal that this causal assertion is "correct," not in that the Western societies show the working example of the ideal, but rather that they reveal either the absence

[7]

or the mongreled and quite unrecognizable shams of these ideals, with the result that the young African mind is disillusioned to an extent far beyond that often recognized. In frustration and disgust with the failures of systems that might have been acceptable were they not blown up out of proportion in propaganda in Africa with the consequent built-up expectation, they pick up a new, powerful, forceful, and almost indestructible strength in their firsthand knowledge of the weaknesses and shortcomings of these Western societies—societies which until now existed almost as a God-realm in the mind of the African at home.

It is this knowledge, this intimate acquaintance with the frailties and weaknesses of what once was an inacessible realm of human purity, this firsthand experience through living and engaging in the daily life of these Western societies, this source of strength, which constitutes the real and final cutting loose of the African mind from the controls of the hitherto oppressor society, and forces it to an almost complete rejection of everything with the slightest identification with that society. This freedom through rejection becomes a necessary prelude to developing an independent mind and thought. It is in this disposition that this younger generation of Africans turns to re-evaluate the entire objectives, goals, and actions of the ruling class at home. And, as much to their surprise as to their disgust, when they, in turn, exhibit those very traits which they resent in the Western society, they experience a shock and disillusionment which together with other related frustrations gather the forces of conflict and revolt to a point of potential explosiveness.

The first response to this is an intensive and highly critical analysis and scrutiny of the existing situation with the consequent determination of what the existent problems are, and what the desirable objectives ought to be, and therefore what changes are necessary to bring about the preferred situation. Having thus, on the basis of whatever theoretical, philosophical, or practical ideas, determined the direction in which they would like to see the continent go, these young men then proceed to face the cold reality of political power and public influence. The first avenue available for bringing about change is, of course, through the polls. But a brief examination of the electoral situation reveals very clearly that the young man, essentially, has little or no chance of ever hoping to offset the power or influence of the deeply entrenched older generation incumbent. The reasons for this are simple. First, the incumbent, in all likelihood, may have been on the band wagon for the struggle for independence. This, of course, gives him the popularity and hero-worship which becomes extremely difficult to fight against. Second, it costs money to go on a campaign and the chances are that the average young intellectual either cannot afford what it would take, or else, in cases of corruption, as happens all over the rest of the world, either his idealism or his peculiar unwillingness to purchase the opportunity to serve his country prevents him from engaging in a figuratively muscular struggle for power with the political veterans. Given then the impossibility of change through the normal process of transfer of political power, the alternatives left are very few indeed.

The young man could either stay in the country and remain either perpetually in the public opposition, probably unelected to a position, or he could allow his frustration to drive him away from the country he so much loves—the country for which he once had and still has so many dreams—the country for which he had dedicated all his academic and intellectual involvement. So now he must pack his bag and baggage and say good-bye to friends and family as he heads for either Europe or some other African country in perpetual self-exile and inevitable eternal disappointment and unfulfillment.

If he does not choose either of these two alternatives, there is only one more avenue left for him, and that is to stand and fight. In other words, the coming into being of revolutionary elements is then clearly a logical result of a vividly perceptible trend of events and not an inordinate occurrence, allegedly inspired by such esoteric suggestions as Communist infiltration or CIA operations. As for the budding revolutionaries themselves, these men are not a bunch of reckless, destructive, youthful rascals who have lost their senses, but a group of highly dedicated young men who are willing to take the obvious risks involved in self-sacrifice for a purpose which is seen as desirable, if not inevitable, for a country and a continent they dearly love.

This then is the process which has led to the contemporary situation in several African countries—simple, straightforward, logical, and far from being amenable to all sorts of fanciful and esoteric theories. This was the situation in Nigeria prior to the First Reaction in January 1966. The young men had absolutely no chance at the polls. They lost heavily to their wealthy, deeply entrenched and often semi-illiterate incumbent rivals. In some cases they faced outright forceful and vicious opponents who could not understand why these "young rascals" would dare oppose such powers as they were. Remarkably, this is precisely the situation which Cyprian Ekwensi most accurately prefigured in his novel *Jagua Nana* which unfortunately seems to have attracted more interest as a story which dramatized the life of a Lagos prostitute rather than the essential point it made of the stiff, almost impossible antagonism that awaited the university trained Nigerian and would-be politician—including the possibility of actual death from the tough thugs of the veteran politicians; remarkable also that when the then Nigerian government refused the filming of the novel it also raised as its objection, not the insight into the political inadequacies of the society, but the impropriety of the dramatization of a prostitute as creating a "bad impression" of Nigeria, not to the Nigerian public (which never seemed to count) but to the outside (Western) world to whom, presumably, prostitution was alien.

This novel, written at a time when one little suspected what was doomed to happen in what was generally acclaimed as the hope of democracy in Africa, whatever the virtue in that was supposed to be, portrayed in all its ramifications the essential patterns that were bound to take place as the younger generation gradually came into the position in which it was bound to expect and demand a hand in the running of the affairs of state. Ekwensi showed an insight into the Nigerian and African political scene that Chinua Achebe and his novel, *A Man of the People,* completely failed to capture even though he was writing his novel many years later, at the point in history when it was obvious to most Nigerians that an uprising of some sort was inevitable.

At this point, it may be pointed out that there existed a close relationship between the young intellectuals and the young officers that led the armed forces. Most of the young university lecturers were at one time or another schoolmates and classmates of the young army officers. Without suggesting a direct plot between these two groups, the fact remained that, as friends and as members of the same generation, and in fact as people who through high school and through the years in the university, at home or abroad, have shared, compared and debated their views on the ideal state they would like to see, there was bound to be a certain common perspective, not only on the existing state of affairs but also on the steps to be taken in bringing about the desired change. In Nigeria, the situation was further aggravated by the outright arrogant indifference of a not insignificant number of the existing political hierarchy. At the time, for example, when most young Nigerians prided themselves on a definite vision for the pan-African movement, the government in power prided itself on a regionalism or nationalism which ran directly against the hopes and expectations of most of its young politically minded population. At a time when most young Nigerians found Kwame Nkrumah, rightly or wrongly, at least the most promising symbol for their future political hopes, the Nigerian government served as the one tool for playing down or outright criticizing the then Ghanaian government, which was particularly significant given the place that Nigeria held on the African continent.

The last straw came when, contrary to the sentiments of the people, certainly of its young generation, and to the expectations, if not the assumptions of all Africa, Nigeria acted at the United Nations to essentially defend (if only by rhetorical avoidance of the direct issue), in essence, the American intervention in the Congo, an act which was obviously highly disapproved of by the rest of the African continent. In so doing, no matter the convictions of the government, it was obvious that it acted contrary to the wishes and opinions of its most vocal and its politically most sensitive, alert, and sophisticated population. It was, therefore, no matter of surprise that all these different elements piled up behind the basic problem of the unwillingness to yield power to a younger generation that also had to play its part in national development; it was not surprising that all of this came to a head and forced the all too-well-known first and supposedly surprising forceful generational showdown in Nigeria—the January 1966 First Reaction.

That the actual execution of that confrontation sparked understandable suspicions and animosities does not in any way make us lose sight of the real forces and issues that led to the conflict in the first place. The purpose of this essay is not to pass judgment on the execution of the First Reaction nor on the desirability of the Second, except to say this much: that it will be tragic if the country and the continent were to lose sight of the very real and very deeply engrained situations and problems that led to that First Reaction. One must confess that it is unfortunate that the execution of that miliary takeover followed a pattern which not only led to the unnecessary killing of many people (especially officers who may not necessarily have been opposed to the struggles of a generation to which they themselves belonged), and from that to the whole chain of regrettable vendettas which have thrown the country into a turmoil of a magnitude unforeseen and most regrettable.

Nevertheless, it will be a bitter disaster if, after all the bloodshed and sacrifice that both sides have had to pay for reason and humanistic pragmatism to succeed temper, inordinate pride and enslavement to relatively trivial technicalities—it will be tragic if after all of this the country returns to precisely the same situation it was in before all the trouble started, with the strengthened presence of all the potential circumstances that led to the conflict in the first place. This will be the case if, after prosecuting the war or running both factions of the country during the times of war, those parties who formed part of that inflexible regime are allowed back into the system, back into their deeply entrenched positions; and if the wishes, enthusiasm, commitment and, in fact, the talents of the younger generation are once again blocked from engaging in the common process of involvement in national development.

It is ironic and a definitely sad commentary on the situation to note that those major figures who have so far lost their lives in the military struggle happen to have been those who seemed most dedicated to serving the unity of the country, no matter the differences in approach; those who were most committed to giving this younger generation a strong hand in running the affairs of a country which, in fact, it is in general better equipped to run. It is in the Nigerian spirit, by which I mean all that has always been Nigerian, including the section now called Biafra, it is, I think, in the best Nigerian spirit, to hope that Banjo, Ifeajuna, and most of all Nzeogu, should not have died in vain.

The death of Nzeogu in itself symbolizes the irony of the struggle. Motivated by the best interests of the country as a whole, he led an action which involved an obvious risk to his life. Apparently forced by circumstances (including his own safety), he fought in a battle which he himself must have hated to see (for who would have thought that he would have dreamed of two factions of the Nigerian army taking up arms against each other), and meeting death at the hands of his former colleagues, he was buried by those who had come to see him as an enemy. I was in Nigeria the night of his death and if one could use the expression, one could say that the profound complexity and irony of the situation was dramatized by the choice of words the commander-in-chief, General Gowon, used to eulogize the national hero. "He was a brilliant soldier," he said. He might have added, "and the bravest Nigerian that ever was."

But beyond and aside from the military personnel involved in the confrontation, there are those originally nonmilitary people, those civilians, who, by virtue of their peculiar position in the society, have been caught in the limelight of the conflict to the regrettable detriment of the important group they represent. All Nigerians, whether Ibo, Yoruba, or Hausa, have always been proud of their writers. Chinua Achebe, Cyprian Ekwensi, and

Christopher Okigbo have always been not only the pride of Nigeria but of all Africa as a whole. Understandable as it may be, one cannot help but regret the fact that the time would ever come when Achebe would have to take a position in London which would necessitate his leading propaganda against a certain faction of the Nigerian people. It is regrettable that Ekwensi would have to leave his position as Director of Information to head an information wing aimed directly at contradicting that which he helped build. I say "regrettable" because I do not for one moment underplay the crucial, complex choices that these men have had to make. I do not choose at this point (or any other) to cast moral judgment on the legitimacy or validity of their decisions. I only say it is regrettable that the choice had to present itself in the first place; that all of a sudden the universality of being Nigerian was reduced to the particularity of being Ibo.

CHRISTOPHER OKIGBO—A MEMORIAL

Most regrettable of all is the fact that one of Africa's best known poets, Nigeria's greatest poet, would have to lose his life fighting a war which did not have to be. All Nigeria, whether on the Biafran side or on the Federal side, and in fact all Africa, if not all humanity, must regret and mourn the untimely and unfortunate death of Christopher Okigbo. No matter our political lineage, we must all bow our heads in solemn remorse and distress at the loss of a life which has been a constant source of inspiration and critical dialogue and debate in African Humanities. This is hardly a fitting eulogy for a man who did not deserve to die, to a heart that always "pulsated with an African sensibility," to use his own words. But perhaps no eulogy is more fitting than to say simply that it behooves all of us to do our best in memory of him to see that he, like the others, should not have died in vain.

THE NIGERIAN PEOPLE—
The Shadow of the Ghost of a Dream

There is no better time to talk about the living than when we remember the dead. It is therefore appropriate at this time when we remember those who so far have lost their lives in the painful experiences of national growth; it is at this time when we remember all the thousands of soldiers and civilians each one of them no less honorable than the men we know and have mentioned by name—it is perhaps at this time that we must also let our thoughts wander to those who are at this point still alive but who remain in constant danger of death as long as civil strife goes on.

It is not the purpose of this essay to pass judgment on the past. Not only would this be irrelevant here, but also this very attitude has been the one major factor in preventing a solution of the present crisis. The situation is at a point where one can conveniently find fault with everyone and when one must therefore appeal to all sides to forget about laying the blame in each other's laps and to bear in mind that the most important issue is the preservation of the most lives in the best circumstances possible. There is no theory, no political objective, no social essence worth greater preservation than humanity itself. It is not worth unity, on the one hand, or secession on the other, if the people themselves do not live to experience the meaning of either.

One must therefore insist that, whatever the political solution to the present crisis, all sides make at least one last genuine effort if only for the sake of the masses of the Nigerian people who have suffered great pains and have borne, with admirable calm, the greatest weight of the conflict in which they have essentially had no say except inasmuch as they have either supported choices made for them or else have tried to make themselves as unobtrusive as possible. At least for the sake of the Nigerian people (and by this I mean the people in all the states of Nigeria, including the East), it is for the sake of these people that one must appeal to the military powers that are to swallow a little bit of their understandable pride and anger, and make one more effort for a peaceful solution of the present crisis.

One need hardly remind one's fellow countrymen, be it General Gowon or Major Ojukwu, that it is an inextricable part of the African Humanism to uphold life and love as being completely transcendental to every other essence which of necessity must hold all but equal importance in the lives of people. It is true, of course, that much has happened to harden the different factions. But if one thinks back a little bit and realizes that after all, only three years earlier many of the officers fighting on both sides were working side by side as colleagues and as partners who would have fought, also side by side, to defend the integrity of Nigeria, then one must allow a little stray speculation that perhaps the differences are not all that insuperable.

It is most regrettable also that those who had to prosecute the war on both sides were those who had no hands in creating the situation that led to the original conflict. It is ironic that, if this conflict were carried to a murdering totality, that generation which sought to find a place for itself in the handling of national affairs would have succeeded remarkably in achieving the absurdity of destroying itself in the process of doing so. This certainly would be a sad commentary on the political, social, and humanistic history of the Nigerian people. This, certainly, is a history Africa did not wish to write—not

[17]

because of what the world might think, which at this point is irrelevant, but because of what it would mean to Africa herself—a legacy unfit to hand down to the generations to come. Perhaps the most convincing reason to bring an end to hostilities was the Nigerian people themselves. In wandering through the streets of Lagos, Ibadan, Benin, Sapele, or Agbor in the initial weeks of the armed conflict, one noticed a disposition which was far from being existent five years before when one left home with the dreams and enthusiasms of going abroad to learn, in order to come back and help, in whatever small way, to build the nation we all could *and still would* be very proud of. In 1962, the Nigerian people were a happy-go-lucky people, always with a smile for every one, a people who danced and whistled and enjoyed a good night at the club after a solid five and a half days of serious work. The Nigerian people were not the frightened, frustrated, disillusioned people they turned out to be in the summer of 1967. The metamorphosis forced a lone reluctant tear that rent a heart to shreds, as the facts had earlier done to a little dream. But it is easy to see what had happened to the people as elite after elite had promised them and had held up a little hope for them, only to disappoint them.

In the present situation, it is hard to see how my generation, that slightly behind the present ruling generation, can ever again hope to serve or lead the Nigerian people when the time comes, because one fears that so much justifiable cynicism and indifference may have been created as to make anyone seem ridiculous in seeking to hold out any hope for the masses of the suffering people. The echo of pessimism is the ghost of a dream that could be born again—perhaps.

The purpose here, of course, is not to blame any of the present rulers for a situation for which all Nigerians must accept responsibility. It is the purpose, however, to plead once again that perhaps the only hope for our and future generations of having the chance to play their legitimate role in the service of their people lies in the ability of the present ruling generation, the present feuding generation, to provide the people with at least a little hope of an end to the seemingly endless chain of promise, hope, disappointment, disillusionment, promise, hope again and yet another disappointment and bigger disillusionment with extreme cynicism as an end product. The Nigerian people do not deserve this. The military leaders do not deserve the responsibility which I am sure they all wish they did not have to bear. But somewhere, somehow, between the people and the leaders, it should be possible to find a solution which would be both realistic and fundamental, and once again rekindle in the big heart of the man in the street a new flame of faith and enthusiasm that will outshine the darkness and gloom of cynicism that sputters hard by.

WOLE SOYINKA:
An Arrest and a Plea

As we have seen, the literary figures, the writers, the university lecturers and the intellectuals have come more into the limelight in the progress of the present crisis. For those of Ibo heritage, they have had to use the prestige which they gained by virtue of their achievements as humanists in situations which have been regrettably, though understandably, propaganda roles. It will be superfluous and unrealistic to blame them for responding to the call in answer to which they actually had no choice. One cannot suggest that the writers shirked their responsibilities and responses when the youngest private has no choice when called to take up arms. One can, however, regret the choice, and in so doing, uphold the superiority of the humanistic concern above the immediate political demands of the situation. It is in this regard that we wish to comment briefly on the arrest of Africa's leading playwright, Wole Soyinka.

While we do not know in detail the reasons for Soyinka's arrest (though we understand from government statements that this is in relation to an alleged conspiracy with fellow Nigerians), we appeal to the Federal authorities and, in particular, the commander-in-chief, General Gowon, to review with us one or two central and pregnant issues with regard to his arrest. It is an African virtue to place purpose and objectives above effort and action. We do not know what specific actions Wole Soyinka may have taken. We do not know; we do not *care* to know. For facts, after all, are just facts. But we can say this much, we are sure that the commander-in-chief will agree with us that in a situation of crisis and, in particular, in the situation in which power and those who hold it change rather rapidly, it takes time to establish that permanent authority which can in turn effectively control or determine the behavior of a people. We think the General has done very well in this respect. It was quite a surprise to find, as I did when I was in Nigeria in August, that the Nigerian people did in fact trust the General, believed in him and looked up to him to do the best he could to solve the not exactly easy problems that faced the nation. It was an experience of extreme pride when I heard him praise Nzeogu in his death and promise him a full military burial as such a national hero deserved. It was the mark of a man of integrity, of a man of unquestionable magnanimity.

It is to these same qualities, therefore, that we appeal in suggesting that Wole Soyinka's case be reviewed, not solely in terms of what specific actions he may have taken or where he may have gone when, but rather on the basis of what his ultimate purpose or objective might have been. We suspect, and are sure the General will agree with us, that this objective could not be anything more than the ultimate solution of the present Nigerian crisis. Admittedly, the government might justifiably feel that the steps he may have taken toward effecting this may have been contrary to the preferences of those in power. But we must not forget that, especially at a time of crisis, there are many people with many different and often conflicting ideas as to how best to achieve the same end. It is at such a time that it becomes extremely important to allow a little leeway, a little flexibility, in overlooking whatever potentially erroneous actions may be taken by individuals in an attempt to achieve a goal which is for the common good. This, I suspect, is the case with Wole Soyinka. As one who knows Wole Soyinka personally, and as one who, in fact, saw him and talked to him in New York only a week before he was arrested, I feel confident in saying that I have no question whatsoever as to his devotion to the country.

I am sure the chief executive will agree with me that this more than at any other time is the moment when we must minimize the sacrifices we have to make in order to solve a situation, the existence of which we all regret. This certainly is not the time to discourage genuine interest and involvement in the search for a solution by frightening all others who would very much want to be involved in the common effort, for fear that their specific actions might be misunderstood and misinterpreted as treasonable. I am sure the commander-in-chief will also agree with me that at the time of military coups and counter-coups the question of treason or treasonable action becomes slightly nebulous and ill-defined, as it is itself part of the general ephemera that are in near constant flux.

This is not to undermine or underestimate the importance of national security, but rather to suggest that it is only too easy, without intending to, to jeopardize the

life, safety, or freedom of some of the best and most devoted citizens out of an honest disregard or misinterpre-
tation of intention. We do not in the least suggest that
the writer be above the rule of law. We do, however,
suggest that more understanding, perhaps, should be
taken in examining the behavior of artistically oriented
people, not only because of their potential idiosyncrasies
which often tend to be misunderstood (and Wole certainly has one or two), but also because it is the creative
artist who, as a committed citizen, will take the chance
of saying things or doing things that many would feel
less willing to risk. This kind of a challenge, this kind of
commitment, this kind of involvement, is one which the
government must encourage.

It is at this time, more than any other, that those in
authority in Nigeria must encourage the young people
to freely say what they think and to offer their opinions
and efforts toward the general national cause. This can
only be done if there is no question whatsoever as to the
good faith of the government with respect to the safety,
security, and freedom of expression of all those who
might otherwise be "sticking their necks out" dangerously
in an attempt to find a solution for the problem which is
as much theirs as anyone else's.

If, however, the government does, in fact, feel strongly
that it has a case against Wole Soyinka regarding his
ultimate intention—that is, if the government feels that in
his action Wole Soyinka did show without doubt that he
did not have the interests of all of Nigeria at heart—if
it feels that it has a pet case too prized to be sacrificed
in gesture of good faith to the many young citizens
whose sentiments it cannot but be sensitive to, then the
government is, of course, free to prosecute him. In that
case, perhaps it would save unnecessary speculation and
unnecessary aspersions cast against the government to
yield to Mr. Soyinka's wife's plea that her husband be

given, an open trial at the earliest possible time. We, however, suggest that if the government does, in fact, find even the slightest element of good intention in the behavior of Mr. Soyinka, the government remember that it is a nobler act to free a man as an act of faith than to bring him to trial on matters of technicalities. Many young Nigerians will always remember the government and praise it, and certainly feel more comfortable about it, if it does demonstrate this good faith. Mr. Soyinka is too valuable a Nigerian to waste away in the confines of his prison cell. It does not matter what the physical environment is. The fact still remains that, as long as he is confined, he essentially cannot perform those functions which he must perform, including the running of the Department of Drama at the University of Ibadan.

Finally, we must note with regret that certain elements of the Nigerian press have felt a compulsion to degrade the unquestionably high quality of Mr. Soyinka's drama by claiming, since he was arrested, that he is, in fact, no more than a mediocre playwright. This reckless trifling with the quality of art is a greater disservice to the country and its people than anything Soyinka or any other Nigerian could possibly have done. It does not matter if it is Wole Soyinka or any other Nigerian writer or artist, since we actually have no personal or particular prejudice in the present situation. But the fact remains that if it can happen to one writer it can happen to any other writer. Will Nigeria go on to say that writer after writer who has unmistakably made his mark in the world of international literature and drama is, after all, worthless because of his alleged political views or actions? Has Nigeria started to disown or degrade her own gems? No. For Nigeria's sake, No! This cannot be. It is not Nigerian. It must not be.

All these questions we raise as we contemplate the role

[23]

of the writer in politics. Nigeria has been our case in point, but there's no reason to suppose that it could not be any other African country the next time around. The crucial issue is and will always remain simply this: that no country, and in particular no African country, can afford to blunt the enthusiasm and involvement, the commitment and devotion of its most sensitive and potentially most useful citizens. It is this group, the young intellectuals, the artists, the writers, the university lecturers and the students in general, who must not be disillusioned beyond the point that is inevitable. The facts of life already take their sizable toll. It is this group that must be encouraged to find some validity in involvement with the pressing issues of national development. It is this group that must be encouraged to freely express its views on the best approaches to the cooperative search for solutions to problems and pressing issues that confront all of us in Africa as individuals and as nations, and be listened to.

Nigeria, like the rest of Africa, needs her young and brilliant minds. The young intellectual, whether writer or engineer, should not and will not operate fully as a tool in the service of the establishment, be it foreign or indigenous. The young African will not invariably aspire to the expectations or demands of the big bosses. This is the cold and happy fact. This we must bear in mind as we prosecute the present crisis in order that those who have sacrificed their lives in the unfortunate service of their country shall not have done so in vain.

Nigerian Fiction and the African Oral Tradition

The following essay is presented in the hope of eliciting responses from African readers and writers about how they perceive African fiction. It is extraordinarily difficult for a person outside the cultural milieu in which literature is created and read to know what the literature means to the readers. Even careful research can lead an outside observer astray because his cultural sights are too narrow. The following comments refer to only one kind of influence on Nigerian fiction, the kind which is usually neglected by non-African literary analysts, and the kind which is most difficult for them to evaluate. The author may be way out on a limb in making some of the statements which follow. If so, she would welcome being pushed off the limb with some specific data based on the experience of African readers and writers.

Nigerian fiction in English has recently attracted considerable attention because of the rapid increase in works available outside Nigeria and the nuances of culture conflict which the fiction depicts. Most often Nigerian fiction is discussed as if it were derived wholly from the English literary tradition of which it is a part. However, the African oral tradition has had great, though not always obvious, influence on Nigerian fiction, even though the content of the fiction may bear little superficial resemblance to that of oral tradition. Critics frequently point out weaknesses in plot and character development in Nigerian fiction, without indicating that plot and characterizations in Nigerian fiction are very similar to those in West African oral literature.

Less than 20 of nearly 350 works of Nigerian fiction in English which have been examined [1] deal with traditional characters in a traditional setting, and seven of these are by one author, Amos Tutuola. The Nigerian fiction which includes traditional characters and traditional settings consists of essentially well-known oral tales which are retold with modern elaborations, or personifications of animal characters. For example, many of the events in Tutuola's stories can be traced directly to Yoruba tales which have been recorded, or have been retold by other writers in both English and Yoruba, thereby indicating that they are a part of the contemporary

[1] This paper is based on research on Nigerian prose fiction in English, which was supported in part by an American Association of University Women fellowship. The 350 works of fiction examined include: novels, short stories, chapbooks and plays written in English. No works written in the vernacular and translated into English were considered in making the generalizations about fiction. The oral traditions used as a basis for comparison were those of the Ibo, Ijaw and Yoruba cultures since the majority of Nigerian writers of fiction are members of these cultural groups.

oral literature.[2] And all the major motifs in Tutuola's stories, like journeys to other worlds, magical transformations, difficult initiations, gaining wisdom through suffering, and so on, are common in West African oral literature, as well as in the oral literature of other parts of the world.

Each of Tutuola's book-length tales is based on a journey to another world from that in which the hero or heroine lives.[3] As might be expected, Tutuola uses in

[2] For example, so many incidents in Tutuola's stories resemble those in the Yoruba tales of Fagunwa that he has been accused of plagiarism. The same tales used by Tutuola have also been retold as fiction in English by Emiko Atimomo, "Forty Days in the Jungle," *Sunday Express* (Lagos), Feb. 28, 1960, p. 12, and A. O. Osula, *The Great Magician* (Zaria: Gaskiya Corporation, 1953).

[3] In *The Palm Wine Drinkard* (London: Faber, 1952) a man goes to Dead's Town to find his palm wine tapper. On the way he goes to the following places, all of which are inhabited by strange creatures: Wraith Island, Greedy Bush, Red Bush, Red Town, Town Where Everyone Walks Backwards, Unreturnable Heaven's Town and Unknown Mountain. In *My Life in the Bush of Ghosts* (London: Faber, 1954) a seven-year-old boy enters the bush of ghosts which is forbidden to humans. He spends 24 years trying to get out and visits 18 towns and other places including: Town of Burglar Ghosts, Bottomless Ravine's Town, Talking Land, Spider's Web Bush, Town of the Short Ghosts, Nameless Town, Hopeless Town, Lost or Gain Valley and Town Where They Worship Mosquitoes. The heroine of *Simbi and the Satyr of the Dark Jungle* (London: Faber, 1955) is kidnapped by a man and taken to Sinner's Town. On her way through the deep jungle she goes to the Path of Death, Town of Multi-Coloured People and The Town Where Nobody Sings. The heroine of *The Brave African Huntress* (London: Faber, 1958) willingly enters the dreaded jungle of the pygmies, from which no one ever returns alive, to rescue her brothers. She also visits The Semi-Jungle, Bachelors' Town, Ibembe Town and Town Under the Rock. In *Feather Woman of the Jungle* (London: Faber, 1962) a man continually seeks wealth and adventure by going to these places, all inhabited by strange creatures or people unlike himself: Bush of Quietness, Town of Famine, Town of Water People, Town of Diamonds, Wells from which Sun and Moon Arise and Town of Wealths.

his tales both familiar items from Yoruba oral literature, as well as local variations of Yoruba oral literature which have not previously been recorded.[4] For example, he explains the presence of universal death as resulting from death having been captured in a net in the land of the dead and taken to an old man in the land of the living. When death is released from the net at the old man's door, it does not know where to go, and so has been running around the world ever since.[5] Tutuola also personifies drum, song, and dance, which use their human capacities to save people from monstrous creatures and severe punishments.[6] Despite the predominantly traditional orientation of Tutuola's stories, their content is marked by European influence that has been interwoven with the oral tradition to create his fantasies which are told in the "best Yoruba tradition." [7]

> Tutuola has been called a great story-teller because: . . . the loose structure of his sentences, his roundabout expressions and his vivid similies, essentially African, remind one very forcibly of the rambling old grandmother telling her tale of spirits in the ghostly light of the moon.[8]

In actual plot structure there is a great similarity between the traditional fantasy tales of Tutuola and novels and chapbooks in English. In each of Tutuola's fantasies, one character travels widely and has many different ad-

[4] Cyprian Ekwensi, "Review of Amos Tutuola: The Palm Wine Drinkard," *African Affairs*, 51, pp. 203–258, 1952.
[5] Tutuola, *The Palm Wine Drinkard*, pp. 9–16.
[6] *Ibid.*, pp. 35ff., 83ff.
[7] This evaluation was made by a university-educated Yoruba, and one of Nigeria's severest literary critics. Wole Soyinka, "From a Common Black Cloth," *AMSAC Newsletter*, 6:5, 1962.
[8] This evaluation was made by a Yoruba writer and critic, in a literary publication directed to an African audience. Mabel Jolaoso, "Review of Amos Tutuola: My Life in the Bush of Ghosts," *Odu*, 1:43, 1955.

ventures, and no minor character has any important role in influencing the development of the plot or in influencing the personality of the major character. In most of the novels (especially those written before 1965) and novelettes, one character experiences the clash of traditional and modern cultures in several different places and in a variety of ways, but no other character emerges as a distinct personality or markedly influences the development of the plot. Both Tutuola's stories and most novels and chapbooks lack extensive description of character, scene, or background to the narrative. Their unity, as in the cycles of West African oral tales, is achieved through the major character who is easily identifiable, even though not described, and experiences a series of actions or adventures in which he is central. Their unity does not derive from any particular logical connection of the many actions included in the plot, nor does it necessarily consist of a unified series of events which lead to a climax.

Likewise, Nigerian short stories resemble traditional West African tales, since they are rarely more than anecdotes, with a specified or implied moral, rather than the stories with a developed plot which are common in the English literary tradition.[9] In the traditional tales, action centered on one person, as in the tale cycles, or on several persons or animals, none of whom was truly dominant. Similarly, in the short stories the action either centers on one person (who often tells the story), or on the action of several persons, none of whom is truly dominant, even though one name may appear in the title of the story. Although some short stories lack the statement of a specific moral lesson at their conclusion, most

[9] Reference is being made to the majority of short stories. Those written by university-educated writers are more likely to have a relatively developed plot although they too may be anecdotal stories, indicating that the difference is not all a matter of training.

have morals which are self-evident to any reader familiar with the setting of the story.[10] Dialogue is frequently used in the stories and other kinds of fiction and sometimes it dominates short stories, but it is purely conversational and rarely reveals the motivations of the characters, or illuminates their personalities. Monologues or descriptions in which characters examine themselves or reflect upon their lives are very rare in Nigerian fiction, except plays.

The emphasis on action and narrative and the relatively infrequent use of description in the fiction does not appear to be a result of lack of writing ability, for some clear verbal pictures have been written by authors trained at the university level and familiar with a wide range of English literature. For example, the sounds of the night are described:

> The world was silent, except for the shrill cry of insects, which was part of the night, and the sound of the wooden mortar and pestle as Nwayieke pounded her foo-foo.
>
> Nwayieke lived four compounds away, and she was notorious for her late cooking. Every woman in the neighbourhood knew the sound of Nwayieke's mortar and pestle. It was also part of the night.[11]

Or feelings may be tersely stated, as in the case of a man who has recently murdered a boy:

> Once he got up from bed and walked about his compound. He felt like a drunken giant walking with the limbs of a mosquito. Now and then a

[10] One example would be David Owoyele, "The Will of Allah," in Frances Ademola (ed.), *Reflections* (Lagos: African Universities Press, 1962), pp. 34–39. Many of Cyprian Ekwensi's short stories, especially those in *West Africa*, are further examples.
[11] Chinua Achebe, *Things Fall Apart* (London: Heinemann, 1958), p. 84.

cold shiver descended on his head and spread down his body.[12]

Since writing good narrative is not emphasized in the English educational system under which the Nigerian writers have been trained,[13] and writers with all levels of education produce works with relatively great narrative emphasis compared to the development of scene and character, this extensive use of narrative has probably been influenced by the oral tradition with which all the writers have been familiar from childhood. Even those writers who use description write stories which are primarily narratives of the traditional type.

There is other evidence of the influence of forms of oral literature in Nigerian fiction, one of the most notable being the use of proverbs. The use of proverbs in fiction is not in itself a distinguishing feature, since proverbs are used in fiction throughout the world. However, traditional proverbs, universal proverbs, and Western wise sayings are used in nearly 80% of Nigerian fiction. Traditional proverbs alone can often be specifically identified in most novels and plays, where there is much dialogue in which they might occur.[14] Although

[12] *Ibid.*, p. 55.

[13] This statement is supported by numerous books and articles including, R. J. Mason, *British Education in Africa* (London: Oxford University Press, 1959), and D. E. S. Maxwell, "English Literature in West African Schools," *West African Journal of Education*, 8,2: pp. 88–90, 1964.

[14] Traditional-sounding proverbs are used frequently, but identifying them *specifically* is quite difficult. Since the traditional proverbs of no Nigerian culture have been fully recorded, exact analogues cannot be found in published collections for all the proverbs. Context is always important in determining what is proverbial, and sometimes context alone determines what is proverbial or what sounds as if it were derived from oral tradition. In many instances it is possible only to indicate a similarity between proverbs in fiction and oral tradition and to suggest that oral tradition is the source. Identification is complicated by the fact that all the authors have had some familiarity with the English literary tradition and

specific frequencies of the use of proverbs in other literature are not available for comparison, proverbs seem to
be rarely characteristic of the whole body of a written
literature, which makes the frequency of their occurrence in Nigerian fiction seem unusually high, especially
since a large number of different authors from diverse
backgrounds and with different amounts of formal education are involved.

Proverbs are an integral part of oral literature, as they
are of West African life. They have also been used in
English literature with varying frequency, depending on
changes in the social environment. They have most often
been used in ages of controversy and satirical criticism,
and are frequently found in literature that characterizes
the folk or appeals to the folk, when appeal to the
fundamental emotions is made, *and during times of
nationalistic and racial striving.*[15] Therefore, frequent
use of proverbs might be expected in Nigerian fiction,
especially because of the controversial nature of the
contemporary Nigerian value system which is developing
through the incorporation of both traditional and
modern elements, and because the social climate is one
of nationalistic striving and the assertion of African
capabilities. The West African oral tradition which used
proverbs extensively in many contexts, in both pointed
and indirect statements, contains much material which
could be utilized in such social circumstances.

In Nigerian novels and plays in which proverbs are
used in greatest concentration, they are most frequently

---

its proverbs. In some instances the proverbial wisdom of the two
traditions is quite similar so that it is impossible to determine the
exact source of the proverbs. For example, a well-known European
proverb that appears in several works of fiction is, "Where there's
smoke there's fire." However, it is very similar to an African
proverb, "The eye which sees the smoke will look for fire."

[15] Archer Taylor, *The Proverb* (Hatboro: Folklore Associates, 1962),
pp. 172–174.

used in village settings, in contexts which refer to criticism of culture change or conflicts of culture values, as well as in traditional ceremonies, greetings, and rites. Chinua Achebe, who makes extensive use of proverbs in his novels, often repeats the same proverbs in several different circumstances and in several different novels. For example, he uses the proverb "When an adult is in the house the she-goat is not left to bear its young on its tether" on four different occasions in one novel: 1) to indicate that people's behavior was cowardly compared to that of their ancestors, 2) to indicate the shamefulness of village elders in allowing one of their clansmen to be killed without demanding retribution, 3) to explain to policemen why the man they are seeking got away, 4) to urge village leaders to stop the spread of fear before it reaches dangerous proportions.[16] Achebe uses proverbs both to give information and to express the motives and thoughts of characters. When a man is deeply in debt and is unable to pay the premium on his car, he rationalizes his inability to pay in terms of the proverb:

> It is not right to ask a man with elephantiasis of the scrotum to take on smallpox as well, when thousands of other people have not had their share of small diseases.[17]

As in West African oral narrative, Achebe also uses a series of proverbs in immediate succession, when a character in a traditional setting is speaking or thinking seriously.

The playwright, Wole Soyinka, uses this same device, as when a man discusses the difficulty of being patient:

> The eye that looks downward will certainly see

[16] Chinua Achebe, *Arrow of God* (London: Heinemann, 1964), pp. 21, 31, 189, 258.
[17] Chinua Achebe, *No Longer at Ease* (London: Heinemann, 1960), p. 98.

the nose. The hand that dips to the bottom of the pot will eat the biggest snail. The sky grows no grass but if the earth called her barren it will drink no more milk. The foot of the snake is not split in two like a man's or in hundreds like the centipede's, but if Agere could dance patiently like the snake, he will uncoil the chain that leads into the dead.[18]

Soyinka also makes use of proverbs in a satirical manner, especially in his play about the meeting of traditional and modern cultures, *A Dance of the Forests,* which he wrote for Nigeria's independence celebrations. Drama, of course, lends itself particularly well to the use of proverbs in dialogue or in a series of questions. Proverbial references can also be based on tales, just as they are in oral literature. For example, a man answers his wife's questions in the following manner:

> They say when the rock hit the tortoise, he shrugged his shoulder and said, "I've always been cracked." When his wife met him, she asked, "When did you begin to clatter?" [19]

To anyone familiar with Yoruba tortoise tales, the origin of this comment is clear, despite its expression in modern idiom.

The same proverbs, both traditional and Western, may be used by different authors, indicating a wide range of applicability of the proverbs, as well as a tendency for the authors to think and express comparisons in terms of proverbs. For example, in the novel, *Blade Among the Boys,* Onuora Nzekwu uses the previously mentioned proverb about the tethered goat to explain why a boy

[18] Wole Soyinka, *A Dance of the Forests* (London: Oxford, 1963), p. 38.
[19] *Ibid.,* p. 41.

[34]

is sent away to live with his grandmother,[20] and Thomas Iguh uses it in a chapbook novelette, *The Disappointed Lover,* when a woman tries to persuade her daughter to tell the truth.[21]

A proverb may also be used as the basis for a recurrent theme without being explicitly stated. For example, Cyprian Ekwensi states that the theme of *Beautiful Feathers* is the following proverb:

> However famous a man is outside, if he is not respected inside his own home, he is like a bird with beautiful feathers, wonderful on the outside, but ordinary within.[22]

This idea is discussed on several occasions in the novel without the proverb being explicitly repeated, although it is clearly implied by the context. Without specifying the proverb, Achebe uses the same theme in *Things Fall Apart,* in a discussion of how a man is not truly a man regardless of his great prosperity if he cannot rule over his wife and children. To a reader familiar with West African oral literature and values, this discussion would probably bring the proverb to mind, and thereby enhance the meaning of the passage; whereas to a reader unfamiliar with the oral literature, the appropriate proverb would not be evoked and the passage might appear to be superfluous explanation, or would be understood only in terms of the literal meaning of the words. Likewise, generalized proverbs like, "The start of weeping is hard," [23] which are common in West African oral

[20] Onuora Nzekwu, *Blade Among the Boys* (London: Hutchison, 1962), p. 127.
[21] Thomas Iguh, *The Disappointed Lover* (Onitsha: A. Onwudiwe, n.d.), p. 49.
[22] Cyprian Ekwensi, *Beautiful Feathers* (London: Heinemann, 1963), p. 1.
[23] Achebe, *op. cit.,* p. 97.

literature, will have more specific connotations for readers familiar with the oral literature.

A common topic of the chapbooks is the many difficulties caused by beautiful women, and the problems encountered as a result of having beautiful wives. A Yoruba proverb used in the chapbooks which would be known to Nigerian readers is, "He who marries a beauty marries trouble." [24] Thus the use of traditional proverbial wisdom in modern settings can be a device for evoking associations with a common theme that may be applicable in both settings, and may enhance the meaning of the less familiar setting. Furthermore, it is not unlikely that when animals which are common in West African oral literature like the dog, chicken, hawk, lion, tortoise, ram, goat, monkey and elephant are used in describing persons or in making comparisons, which they commonly are in Nigerian fiction, their proverbial implications will be evoked for those familiar with oral literature. (Field research is essential for determining the kind and extent of such associations which Nigerian readers make.)

As indicated in the preceding examples, the extensive use of proverbs seems to be an important aspect of Nigerian fiction. Whether the proverbs can be recognized as traditional: "Let the hawk perch and the eagle shall perch. Whichever bird says to the other, 'Don't perch,' let its wings break," [25] or are derived from Shakespeare, "The evil that men do must continue to live after them," [26] or are universal, "He who waits will see what is in the grass," [27] may be significant in determining the

[24] Selwyn Gurney Champion, *Racial Proverbs* (New York: Barnes and Noble, 1963), p. 607.
[26] Thomas Iguh, *Alice in the Romance of Love* (Onitsha: Providence Printing Press, n.d.), p. 10.
[25] Nkem Nwankwo, *Danda* (London: Andre Deutsch, 1964), p. 13.
[27] Cyprian Ekwensi, *Burning Grass* (London: Heinemann, 1962), p. 63.

[36]

sources of inspiration and the originality of the individual authors. However, to the Nigerian reader, if proverbs or other elements of oral literature appear to be authentic in the context of the story or are meaningful to the readers as such, then for all practical purposes, they are folklore and serve similar functions in the fiction. Where conversation in proverbs seems natural, the tales told at the fireside by fictional characters are familiar, and the themes of incidents are those commonly portrayed in oral literature. Folklore of tradition is a coherent part of the fiction so far as the Nigerian reader is concerned.

Several novels which have contemporary settings incorporate traditional tales in the context of their plots. The tales are always told in village settings as a group is seated around a fire or by an old woman or a mother to a child. These are the same situations in which tales are really told, and in fiction they are used to illustrate a moral about some culture conflict which has occurred in the plot of the story.

Epigrammatic naming which is similar to the praise names of oral literature is frequently used in Nigerian fiction. It is used in traditional situations, as in a modern version of a Hausa tale where a town is called "The Land Where Everyone Holds Himself In a State of Readiness," and its leader is "The Sorrow in Your Heart Is Little." [28] Derivatives of praise names are also used in the same situations in which they are used in contemporary Nigerian life, especially to name lorries and cars: "The Chimney of Ereko," "God My Saviour," "Trust No Man," and "God's Case No Appeal," for example. The frequent use of epigrammatic naming probably derives from the oral tradition, as it is uncommon in the English literary tradition.

[28] Cyprian Ekwensi, *An African Night's Entertainment* (Lagos: African Universities Press, 1962), pp. 34–35.

[37]

Praise names are also applied to items of particular significance, like a double spring bed which is called "Holy of Holies," [29] or used to designate personal qualities of an individual, like a beautiful pious girl whose name is "Comfort," [30] or the wicked "Mr. Monger," who forbids his daughter to marry.[31] Nicknaming is also common, especially in the chapbooks, to designate a person's qualities, as the proud girl who is dubbed "Peahen of West Africa," [32] and the maker of love charms who is called "Put Me Among Girls." [33] Praise names are commonly used for similar purposes in West African oral literature. They are a brief way of describing persons, places, and things, so that their frequent use in fiction which is largely narrative adds a descriptive dimension which would otherwise be lacking.

These examples and others which could be cited indicate that West African oral literature has had extensive influence on Nigerian fiction in English, despite its dominant concern with contemporary life. The primarily narrative nature of the fiction can be traced to the oral tradition, as can the use of proverbial references and praise names for description and the use of proverbs and tales for providing commentary on the actions of the characters. These aspects of African oral literature are important influences on the way in which Nigerian authors develop their stories and the way in which the fiction is understood by different segments of the Nigerian audience and by European audiences.

[29] Achebe, *op. cit.*, p. 14.

[30] C. N. Aririguzo, *Miss Comfort's Heart Cries for Tonny's Love* (Onitsha: Aririguzo and Sons, n.d.).

[31] Okenwa Olisah, *About Husband and Wife Who Hate Themselves* (Onitsha: Eastern Niger Printing Press, n.d.)

[32] Cletus Gibson Nwosu, *Miss Cordelia in the Romance of Destiny* (Port Harcourt: Good Will Printing Press, n.d.), p. 12.

[33] Ogali A. Ogali, *Okeke the Magician* (Aba: Okeudo and Sons, n.d.), p. 10.

Recent Developments in French African Literature

by PAULETTE J. TROUT

The literature of French-speaking Africa has been in a state of transition for the past five years. In adapting to the post-colonial era, the themes of rebellion and revolt have disappeared. As a prominent former African poet and present politician explained to this editor, many poets have chosen "the narrow gate" (to paraphrase Gide) and have taken the more pragmatic path of politics, leaving the muses for their retirement years.

In "La grande misère de la littérature Négro-Africaine," (*Jeune Afrique,* 12 September 1965), the Senegalese Signaté Ibrahima perceptively explains how in general the African author today is of little influence in his homeland and so writes primarily for a foreign public. This point is noted again in *France-Eurafrique* (1965) when Urbain Dia-Moukori asks for whom the

[39]

writers of today really write. A return to African sources in order to develop traditional themes that would give these works an authentic African flavor, as done by such writers as Birago Diop and Bernard Dadié, is the advice given by Mohamadou Kane in "L'Ecrivain africain et son public" (*Présence Africaine,* n° 58, 2e trimestre 1966). Mohamadou Kane, who teaches literature at the Faculty of Letters at Dakar, points out that Anglophone literature has had an acute sense of reality that has given it an extraordinary vitality. Furthermore, the English-speaking writers tend to be more in communion with their audiences. Kane recommends less ostentatious rhetoric and return to traditional sources.

Negritude or "anti-Negritude" still commands a considerable amount of attention. Among recent essays, one should note Abida Irele's "Negritude: Literature and Ideology," in the *Journal of Modern African Studies,* III (1965) iv, 499-526. Though the theme of Negritude in the African novel has not as yet been extensively examined, E. Makward discusses the subject in *Ibadan,* n° 22 (1965), pp. 37-45 in his article "Negritude and the New African Novel in French," just as does Jean Mayer in his "Le roman en Afrique noire Francophone et l'aventure d'une race" in *Annales de l'Université d'Abidjan,* Lettres et Sciences Humaines, n° 1 (1965), pp. 5-16. Three other essays on Negritude that should be noted are: Feuser, W., "Negritude—The Third Phase," in *New Africa,* V (1965), pp. 63-64, and Triulzi, A., "Il problema della negritude" in *Rivista de sociologia,* VII (1965), iii, pp. 5-50, and Jacques Bolle's "Negritude" in *International African Forum* I (1965), xii, pp. 37-42; II, i, pp. 30-33.

While there have been relatively few works of poetry actually published within the last two years, one should take note of the special issue of *Présence Africaine,* n° 57 (1965) containing an anthology of recent poetry by

Negro authors from Africa and the Americas, with brief introductions and biographical notes by Léon Damas, "Nouvelle somme de poésie du monde noir." Also to be noted is Thomas Melone's "New Voices of African Poetry in French" in *African Forum* I (1966) iv, pp. 65-74. Max Bilen considers the relationship between poet and public in *Présence Africaine* n° 54 (1965), pp. 137-141; and Daniel Abasiekong devotes a few perceptive pages on the Malagsay Poet Rabearivelo in "Poetry Pure and Applied" in *Transition,* n° 23 (1965), pp. 5-48. A short book, useful as a school text and containing a bibliography and cursory notes is Clive Wake, (editor), *An Anthology of African and Malagasy Poetry in French* (London: Oxford University Press, 1965).

There has been little attention given to the difficulties encountered by the student of African literature. Lylian Lagneau Kesteloot fills this gap with her customary insight in her article entitled "Problems of the Literary Critic in Africa," in *Abbia* (Yaoundé), n° 8 (February-March 1965), pp. 29-44.

The novel has received perceptive treatment from Judith Gleason: "The African Novel in French" in *African Forum* I, iv (Spring 1966), pp. 75-92, as well as in her authoritative volume entitled *This Africa, Novels by West Africans in English and French* (Evanston, Illinois: Northwestern University Press, 1965).

Finally, two other recently published original works should be mentioned. One is the novel *Violent était le vent* (Paris: *Présence Africaine,* 1967), by the Ivoirian author Charles Nokan. Nokan illustrates the theme of spiritual uprooting in tones which remind one of the brilliant work by C. Hamidou Kane, *L'Aventure ambigue*. He raises overtones of social anguish, and his style is remarkably poetic and expressive. Another work of note belongs to the theater. Cheik A. N'daor's *L'Exil du roi Albourri* is a historical drama on the nineteenth-century Sudanese Kingdom of Djoloff. As the enemy advances, it is questioned whether one should negotiate or fight, risk death or flee and survive. The author, winner of the 1962 *Prix des poètes sénégalais,* has written a moving and sober piece whose characters are truly individual. N'daor's play forms the first volume of the collection "Théâtre Africain" published in 1968 in Paris by Pierre-Jean Oswald.

Letters from Africa

by JOSEPH OKPAKU

In the summer of 1967 I made a tour of Africa which took me through Senegal, Ivory Coast, Ghana, Nigeria, Cameroun, Congo (Brazzaville), Congo (Kinshasa), Uganda, Tanzania, Kenya, and Ethiopia. Between giving lectures, talking to young African writers and artists and promoting the *Journal* I tried to sense what it was to be back home after five years. It was, of course, good to be home again, but it was not exactly "home sweet home." Some of the experiences were recorded in letters written, during the trip, to a friend. Three of these letters are reproduced below in the belief that they portray, in a personal way, some of the sentiments as they were felt at the time, without the conscious or unconscious censorship that would tend to accompany a direct essay on such subjects as covered here. If some of these sentiments sound lofty, perhaps it is the immediacy of the experience of them.

In order not to disguise this immediacy I have preferred not to edit this selection. The dashes only represent private remarks of the nature of messages or instructions which do not add to the experience. At the risk of being misinterpreted, I have also preferred not to offer any explanations of the content of this selection, except to state that I had been made to understand that the war in Nigeria would break out precisely when it did, and was advised to remain in Paris for a while, especially in the light of stories of students returning home to Nigeria on vacation during the second coup d'état who ran into trouble at the airport. The other letters need no explanation.

15.50 G.M.T.
4th July, 1967
PARIS—LAGOS

Dear Laura,

In about half an hour we shall be landing in Lagos. That it has been an inexpedient decision to go home at this time, there is no doubt. But that it is a valid decision, that's anybody's to judge. I have watched the news carefully in the past couple of days and all indications are that civil war is a foregone conclusion—in fact, violence has already broken out. There were two acts of sabotage in Lagos yesterday, one at the police headquarters in Obalende, a few blocks from my uncles' residences. A family of 4 was killed in their sleep. This morning in Paris I still wasn't sure if I was doing the right thing. In fact I'm still not sure. I called O— at 8 a.m. to check for the latest news and then it dawned on me that a couple of months ago in Los Altos Hills I had actually dreamt of being in Paris waiting to go to Nigeria and hearing reports of sabotage and calling a friend to check out the latest reports.

But in 27 minutes I will be in Lagos—I'm looking forward to it—not with thrill or excitement—which is what it would have been—but with the calm sober consciousness of stepping knowingly into a state of emergency—with a cold chilling awareness that the slightest whim of any one of the men in uniform at the airport could put a rather remarkable end to the throbbing excitement of an interesting life.

It is not the feeling of a martyr, certainly not the bravado of a hero standing on a rolling cart as it clanks its way slowly towards the towering and imposing coldness of the guillotine. Nor is it fear, I'm not afraid. I have been for brief moments in the past several weeks—much more so in the past several days—but I'm not afraid. I have not been since I boarded this plane ½ hour late at Le Bourget this morning. No—it's not fear. Not that I know what it is—not that it matters what.

I guess it is a little disturbing to have to admit the absurdity of the dilemma—which perhaps it is—or rather, the contradiction that there is nothing in this world that could bring me greater joy at this time than the reality of going home—I don't mean to sound like the going back to the roots of our friends of rue Descartes —and yet, there is nothing as risky at this point, as going home.

Perhaps it is this very contradiction that made me decide to go home. I could find all kinds of reasons—not that it matters.

Attachez Votre Ceinture—that's the sign on the wall on the right. I guess we are only 9 minutes from home. Who would have thought that the idea of attaching a safety belt would ever some day hold a frightening symbolism.

But I look forward to it. To being home—to being

[45]

in Nigeria once more. It's been five years. It's been a long time. I look forward to it. Who can blame me for it?

In a few minutes the huge D.C.8 will swoop down on Ikeja airport. How I've longed for this. To be home again, if only for a few days. It was an unwise decision —who will tell me what wisdom is?

We are about to land now—hmm—you know—it's rather funny—who would ever have thought that the time would come when I would have second thoughts about returning home. I have great trust in my people—despite the facts—in spite of them. It is raining, I think. I've always loved to walk in the rain. It rained when I left —no—it isn't raining.

The sun is shining—very bright in fact.

In a few minutes I'll be on Nigerian soil—and in 48 hours or less I'll see Grandma again. I have to. There's nothing anyone can do about it—dead or alive. I have to. I think a cloud stands between me and home—but the sun shines through somehow—and somehow I must —I don't know.

Perhaps nothing will happen—No. Nothing will. But there are accidents and scattered incidences. You know, I don't like to die a silly accidental death—like from being in the neighbourhood of a car loaded with explosives.

Five years ago Nigeria was the safest place on earth— and I loved it then. Five minutes ahead, I fear it is the one place not to be in. But it's home and I love it.

Have I been talking about death? That's what has happened to Nigeria—that's what—no, it can't—that's what I hope doesn't happen to me.

Love,
Joe

P.S. I'll drop a card each day, check the dates just in case.

On back of envelope:
No, there's no rain. I wish there were. The forest is as
green as ever, the stream winding and moody—we'll
land any minute. For the first time today I'm elated.
Just a little bit—it's green and fresh all over. It looks
so peaceful—yes, peaceful. That's the Nigeria I left. God,
I wish it were raining. The creaking of the leather seats
does sound like a drizzle. We're landing now, we have,
God, it's raining. I'm happy. Yes, I am. I'm disturbed,
that's true too.

5:30 p.m. I think we're landing just about the same
time we took off in 1962. It's foggy and gloomy just like
before. There's a quiet thrill—the same as 5 years ago.
Anxiety and expectancy.

En Route BOAC
LAGOS—LONDON (to N.Y.)
July 10, 1967

La Plus Chère Laura,

This trip continues to be one in which all hope of
having some time to rest or write are invariably doomed
to frustration. The only opportunity to do either, it
seems, is on the plane. It is certain now that I cannot
keep a journal of this trip, not in the form of a daily
account. If there is ever a desire to write about it, it
would be as a recollection which is not necessarily less
satisfactory.

We landed in Lagos in the rain, and between swift
glances to take in an overall picture of the location of
soldiers just in case fighting broke out at the airport, I
tried to prepare myself mentally for handling any situations that might arise—especially as a result of the
emergency. Being thus busily engaged, I had no time to
consider, or rather, to reflect upon the problems of ad-
justments arising from my 5 year absence. Consequently

[47]

when I finally took care of everything I was already in Nigeria, living in Nigeria once more and arguing with the cab driver who, like in Paris, charged me exorbitantly.

The situation at the airport was regrettable, regrettable because it was amusing and yet I couldn't laugh.

It started at the health check point. As I handed my papers to the young gentleman who was convincing in the manner in which he took his time, I heard someone whisper—"This one na from Biafra"—which got me rather worried. You will recall that my greatest apprehension was that it was a good chance I could be mistaken for an Ibo (not that I would normally care) and roughed up for that reason. Luckily, one fellow looking at my passport over the slow coach asked if I was related to my uncle (who was once a Senior Superintendent of Police) and that at least seemed to set the records straight —for my interest that is. (Perhaps I should mention that no one was roughed up at the airport though there were scarcely any Ibo around.)

The first re-association with home came shortly after when I proceeded towards the immigration. "This Way! This Way!" I calmly remembered that an interesting characteristic of Nigerian youth, or perhaps any other youth, is the constant presence, in appreciable minority, of those whose self-actualization depends solely on being able to publicly put someone else down, preferably someone of some apparent importance, under the guise of executing their official duty. Once again, I was too tired and too concerned with getting out of the airport fast to even respond.

At the immigration I was told my passport had not been stamped on my way out of Nigeria in 1962. I had decided to say as little as possible, certainly not argue, and to co-operate—even to the point of naiveté if necessary.

[48]

There were 2 reasons for this: first, in realization of the onerous responsibility the situation places on the military; and also because of a frightening appraisal of the dangerous uncertainties of arming young men shortly after enlistment—young men who might place great importance on the novelty of authority backed by gun powder. There was always the possibility of getting shot by an overzealous or hysterical soldier who might mistake an explanation for an argument and might be apt to see a concerted effort to flout his authority in every move one took, especially if one, by virtue of his dress or language and his arrival from overseas, were automatically classified with a snobbish elite. The whole atmosphere, the effort to make things as simple as possible, to obey rather than explain, to hide any irritation no matter how justified, the entire effort, compounded by the seasonal high humidity (it was like Chicago in summer) was quite exhausting.

All this time I was trying to determine who was military and who wasn't. Those with arms seemed easy to identify, except that the police were now also armed. But there was a group in white shorts and shirts with navy blue epaulettes bearing the Nigerian coat of arms— so I thought—By virtue of their unusual smartness—they were much more lively than the obvious soldiers—I figured they might be with the Navy. On the whole they seemed less tense, and naturally I tended to drift towards them.

"Is dis your box? Open it." Behind this man, who must have learnt that all soldiers have a characteristic sternness, was a notice requesting all passengers to please co-operate with the military. Then began the gruelling search. Every silly little thing was examined —which was all right. Then a senior officer came up to me. (By the way, the smart fellows in white were Nigerian Airways [civilian] personnel.)

"What is—in this box?"

"I have already checked it, sir," the private said.

"It is a movie camera lamp," I explained.

"Open it."

So I did.

"Where is the battery?"

"It doesn't use a battery."

"It must use a battery. Where is the battery?"

By now all I wanted to do was hit the sack. I was as indifferent as I was tired.

"It uses," I had to risk an explanation as the situation was getting frightfully tense.

"It is electric, sir," another soldier explained.

"I know, don't tell me." . . (Sorry, sir) . . —"All I want is the battery!"

Since words no longer served in the realm of communication I tried the next best thing—silence. The second private seemed to have a sense of humour which threatened to implicate him when he laughed as he started to say:

"Sir, these things don't. . ."

"Don't tell me what I know."

Meanwhile I drifted away, wondering how one could expect to detect dangerous weapons etc. if a military officer had so much difficulty. Actually it was a most amusing situation, but I didn't dare laugh—not with a gun in the officer's hands.

But silence also failed. So in a last effort I resorted to pantomime without music—I took the plug in my hand and held it up to him.

"You plug it in."

And as it dawned on him what it was I had been trying to convey to him I felt the urge to risk a little explanation as much for my amusement as for his interest. "You plug it in here," I repeated. "And you switch it here."

"And where is the camera."

For the fourth time I said, "I lost it in Paris."

"What is this?"

Quite frankly I had forgotten all about the first private who in the meanwhile had worked his way down to the bottom of the suitcase. He was holding up one of the several boxes of slides.

"Slides," and I offered to open it. In the heat of the confusion I had unconsciously become very relaxed and at home. I offered the gentleman one slide.

"Is it used?" he asked, as he held it up against the light.

"Used? . . . eh . . . " I really didn't know what he could possibly have meant.

"Is it used?" He was rather sterner now, which really no longer bothered me.

"If you mean whether or not I have shown it before, yes."

"All I want to know is if it is used."

As it finally dawned on me that perhaps he thought the slide in his hand, a slide with a picture that was very visible in colour, was something yet to be loaded into a camera and shot—I hesitated before proceeding to risk an explanation.

"All you do is place it in front of a lamp and the picture appears on a screen," an explanation which another private echoed to the strong resentment of the first.

"That's not what I meant."

But it seemed he was answered, thank goodness, and now I had to give good reasons why my movie camera was not there—

As I rode into town later that evening, which incidentally was the 4th of July, I couldn't help smiling at the recollection of the airport episodes. It was not their lack of knowledge of the gadgets that I found amusing, but the anger and irritation with which they betrayed their not unjustifiable ignorance of things no one really need know anything about—funnier still was the ridiculousness of my position, being practically bullied for what couldn't really be called my fault.

But meanwhile I was unconsciously making another readjustment—this time to the roads and traffic.

Perhaps I should mention that there was another military check at the exit of the airport, but the taxi driver, who practically forced me into his beat-up car which had to be pushed to start—and it seemed like a normal routine with him—was an expert on the emergency situation, as indeed all cab drivers must needs be since they, their cars, and their passengers are searched every so often—so we didn't have to go through much.

But back to the traffic. One thing was certain. If I had rented a car at the airport, it was a rather fairly good chance that I would have either crashed the car or killed some people or perhaps both. And if you asked me what judgment I'd place on this—simply, it is a compliment to the Nigerian drivers.

I kept dodging to the left, from my position on the back seat. The rule, after the fact, seemed simply "Drive down the middle of the road, until 3 feet from an oncoming vehicle, then dodge—" And as an afterthought, "the ditches on the left are perhaps preferable." Which seemed to ignore the numerous pedestrians, i.e. those who were not defying the lorries on the middle of the road.

But meanwhile, as I took in the profound expertise of all four—the pedestrians, the drivers, the vehicles, and the roads—I was making yet another readjustment—this time to the physical environment. The rather run down houses interspersed with impressive mansions—the roadside stall (I longed to stop the cab and buy some akara or roasted corn—the smell was irresistibly inviting)—

the relatively inadequate clothing of the people and interestingly, the sudden preponderance of black people like me, with relatively no white person in sight. (I couldn't tell if it was this or the rain and clouds that gave a rather dark (literally only) impression.)

But I got to Lagos all right after another military check and after consciously allowing myself to be cheated by the cab driver who must have thought he either had a foreigner or a rich man at his mercy. He charged £3.10 (He was making a concession he said) while the fare was only £1.10 actually. It was now late at night after two hours on the road and, together with the virtual curfew and the rain that was soaking through my mohair suit, I resigned myself to being cheated.

We are landing in London now—so—Au revoir.

Love,
Joe

P.S. Leave Sunday for Kampala, will leave Kampala for Copenhagen—Dar etc.

August 10, 1967

Air Mail: Accra—Doula

Dear Laura,

You must have heard by now that Ibos in the Mid-West branch of the Nigerian army mutinied and joined Eastern Nigerian troops to capture Benin and other parts of the Mid-West. This afternoon just before leaving Accra we heard Ojukwu's planes have attacked Lagos. I have people in Lagos, my sisters are in Agbor, on the road from Asaba to Benin, which is how the E.N. troops got to Benin and, no doubt, Sapele must have been attacked.

What's there to say? The past 3 weeks in Africa have been one constant trend of disillusionment, anger and pain. Now, I fear, my feelings almost border on indifference, not to the utterly crushing experience but to the passions and emotions of my experience. Is my family safe? I don't know. I have no way of finding out. I hope they are. I pray they are. God, if they are not—what shall I do? Yesterday, when I heard the news of Benin I wanted to change my plans and fly into Lagos —but W. C. advised otherwise. "It's no use, man." That's all he said. True, it's no use. So we went to the Lido for a beer.

We've been flying over the clouds that enshroud Nigeria. It's about 4:30 p.m. sunny and bright. And looking out of the window, one sees scattered ridges with remarkably mushroom shapes, reaching on towards the inaccessible skies, blue and beautiful and below us it is a thick mist, rugged and beautiful. Now and then the silver wings of our propeller plane disappear from our view, lost in the silvery totality of pockets of transient clouds. Below all of this lies a throbbing heart, scattered, bombed, and torn. Below there lies my country—ugly, scared and meaningful. And between us lies a layer of cloud—between me and my family lies a ghastly uncertainty. The cloud shades from me all that's meaningful to me—all that I've always longed to embrace, all that has only recently disillusioned me—all that could destroy me, if I did not believe. But in spite of it all, I must fly above the clouds, no matter how clumsily. I must carry on and once in a while retire into the transient mists, to recuperate and build up my resistance, and return once more, if only to be disillusioned again.

We are in the Cameroons now and will be landing soon in Doula. It is early dusk and outside lie scattered patches of dark green amidst the general light green.

We have landed. I have no passions. I leave for Brazzaville tomorrow morning you know. What has happened
to my family? I do not know. I hope they are safe. They
have to be.

Love,
Joe

Achebe's Christ-Figure

by DONALD J. WEINSTOCK

Young Ikemefuna's active role is over and done with less than a third of the way through Nigerian author Chinua Achebe's splendid first novel, *Things Fall Apart*.[1] Yet it is a part of the story that somehow remains with readers long after they have finished the novel. When a skillful novelist or dramatist eliminates as potentially major and interesting a character such as this so early in a work, he generally has a valid artistic reason for doing so. Achebe does away with Ikemefuna in order to use him to foreshadow the impact of Christianity upon Iboland.

This aim of Achebe's seems to have been overlooked for two reasons: Because his method is as much symbolic

[1] London: Heinemann, 1958; references in the text are to the Heinemann African Writers Series edition, 1962.

as realistic, and because readers do not expect him to be saying what he does say. Many still prefer to read into this novel only the nostalgia for traditional Ibo ways and not the criticism of them, and only the drawbacks and not the benefits of the new customs, values, and religion brought by the white men. To read *Things Fall Apart* in this way is to ignore or distort the artistry its pages reveal.

Even some who perceive that Achebe does not see the world in unrealistically extreme terms fail to realize that he makes value judgments, takes sides. I should like to examine here in some detail one of the many symbolic patterns used in the novel to support what it says in other ways, and which go further than those other ways in evaluating the relative worth of old and new modes of life. Whether or not the author was aware of these judgments is irrelevant so long as the novel makes them. This, I think, can be shown.

Ikemetuna, who comes to Umuofia as a sacrifice and is later sacrificially slain, is clearly one of the multitude of Christ-figures in modern fiction. Achebe unobtrusively draws several parallels between his young character and Jesus. As is common with this device in contemporary novels, each strand of the parallel is by itself admittedly tenuous and approximate. Cumulatively, however, they are impressive.

Like Christ, Ikemefuna comes from one realm to another and is associated with a young virgin (p. 10). He arrives in Umuofia just before the planting season (p. 24), surely the equivalent of Spring, the time of Christ's birth in the flesh. Ikemefuna too is sent to his new destination as a sacrifice, a peace-offering "to avoid war and bloodshed" (pp. 6, 8–10). He helps keep peace also, as when he prevents some of Okonkwo's younger sons from revealing a sister's misdeed (p. 38). (The later

[57]

prevention of violence by Mr. Kiaga and Mr. Brown links Ikemefuna's behavior with those of other, more obviously recognizable, representatives of Christianity [pp. 145, 159].)

Ikemefuna, like Jesus, is only temporarily in the new place. During his stay there he is admired by all who know him. Nwoye likes him because "he seemed to know everything"; the hard-to-please Okonkwo likes him (without showing it very much) because he seems to embody all the manly virtues and is a good influence on Nwoye; others merely like him (pp. 24, 45–46). And, as Christ belongs to all mankind, Ikemefuna "belonged to the clan as a whole" (p. 10; and again on p. 12).

Like Christ, who referred to Himself in organic images and who is often identified with a growing vine or with the Tree of Life, Ikemefuna "grew rapidly like a yam tendril in the rainy season, and was full of the sap of life" (p. 45). The Yam, with which Ikemefuna is also explicitly identified in this passage, is, for the Ibos, "the king of crops," and it "stood for manliness" (pp. 28–29; also p. 19).

Unlike Christ, Ikemefuna never lives to fulfill his earthly promise. He dies at the wrong time of year, "in the cold harmattan season after the harvests had been gathered" (p. 47), in contrast to Christ, whose mortal death was in the Spring, the season of rebirth. Achebe has not slipped; there is a structural reason for this too: Ikemefuna lives among the Umuofians at too early a time in their history to be received properly. After Ikemefuna's linking with "the king of crops," and with an unseasonal death, a prior agricultural description is seen to have metaphorical significance: During Okonkwo's first year on his own farm, he diligently plants a number of seed-yams. As with Ikemefuna's life, however, "nothing happened at its proper time; it was either too early or too late" (p. 19). Okonkwo sows with the first rains, but the fierce sun unseasonally returns and burns up all he has planted. The rains come again, and he sows his borrowed reserves, only to have many of these washed away. Some remain in the ground, but the rain continues "without a pause. The spell of sunshine which always came in the middle of the wet season did not appear. The yams put on luxuriant green leaves, but every farmer knew that without sunshine the tubers would not grow" (pp. 19–20).

Rain, and water in general, is used throughout to represent Christianity; sunshine is part of the fire imagery consistently associated in the novel with traditional religion.[2] Neither the old way nor the new is alone sufficient. By itself, each is destructive; in the right combination they yield sustenance to the community. By the time he is killed, Ikemefuna has had enough rain, for he had grown "rapidly like a yam tendril in the rainy season" (p. 45). But, at the scene of his execution, the sun cannot break through sufficiently; it is partially obscured by the trees overhead (p. 51).

Most significant of all the Christ parallels is Ikemefuna's death and its effect on others. Although he is loved and respected by those with whom he comes in contact, he is sentenced to death by the local equivalents of the biblical high priests who allegedly condemned Jesus—the clan's elders, who are also for the most part its religious leaders (pp. 78–83). The boy walks to his place of execution with those who are to slay him. "The kind of story Nwoye liked best" (with its reference to a religious sacrifice), which precedes the account of Ikemefuna's death by only a few pages, and is separated from it only by another symbolically Christian incident,

---

[2] These matters are explicated in detail in one of a number of forthcoming articles, some in collaboration with C. M. Ramadan. I am also indebted to Mrs. Ramadan for valuable comments relevant to the current essay.

clearly indicates that the death is a sacrificial one in more senses than one.

On the way to be legally murdered, Ikemefuna, like Jesus, carries a burden, a pot of wine, which obviously suggests Christ in a number of ways. The pot falls and breaks as he is struck down. The first blow fails to kill Ikemefuna, and he calls out to Okonkwo, whom "he could hardly imagine . . . was not his real father" (p. 51): "My father, they have killed me!" (p. 53)—words reminiscent of Christ's appeal on the Cross before His death. Whereupon Okonkwo, "dazed with fear, . . . drew his machete and cut him down" (p. 53). Ikemefuna, like Christ, has been betrayed by one whose first charge should have been his safety, one with whom he has eaten from the same bowl (e.g., p. 47). In all these parallels Okonkwo exhibits behavior attributed to Judas in one or another of the Gospels. Like Judas, Okonkwo is seriously distraught after his act of treachery, and, again like Judas, later hangs himself.

Ikemefuna's major influence on Umuofia comes, as did Christ's on the world, after his death. Even this is carefully led up to by Achebe, for we are told almost at the beginning of the novel that "the lad's name was Ikemefuna, whose sad story is still told in Umuofia unto this day" (p. 10; also see p. 6). The "unto" might be a slim clue to the biblical nature of his "sad story," for Achebe generally shuns archaisms. Of Ikemefuna's happy years in the clan, we learn that "Nwoye remembered this period very vividly till the end of his life" (p. 30). Ikemefuna is aware of his impending death (p. 50), as Christ was of His. Finally, Nwoye is emotionally distraught as soon as he becomes aware that Ikemefuna has been killed (p. 53), just as the disciples were after Christ's death. Nwoye apparently continues to ponder the deed and the reasons for it, for his questioning

of its justice is one of the major reasons for his accept-
ance of Christianity (p. 132).

Of course Ikemefuna is neither Christ nor a Christian;
he is dead long before the white missionaries begin to
arrive. But he strongly anticipates the Christ to come
in much the same manner that David—Jesus' ancestor
according to the Gospels—is said to prefigure Christ, in
a commonplace of medieval typology, which sought and
found New Testament figures and events foreshadowed
in the Old Testament.

The implications of this interpretation for the novel
as a whole are obvious. These symbolic suggestions,
linkings, and identifications function structurally to illustrate the limitations of Okonkwo's character. In another sense, they clarify the limitations and the future
history of his entire people. On the one hand, Okonkwo
and Umuofia provide shelter and security of a sort for
Ikemefuna as they do for their own people. On the other
hand, a human being who would obviously have become a valuable citizen is murdered for vague and inadequate religious reasons. Ikemefuna's death reminds
us, as it does Nwoye, of other fruitless killings—those of
twins, for instance—committed with the sanction of the
entire society. These futile murders are doubly harmful;
if Ikemefuna is any example, the community is depriv-
ing itself of incalculable contributions to its life. This
butchering of the young metaphorically expresses the
clan's distrust of youth except in "approved" and hence
rather rigid forms.

Okonkwo represents the narrowness of tribal life carried to an extreme even for his time and place. His
friend Obierika is flexible enough to question the justice of traditional ways and to wonder how laws change
(pp. 61, 111–112). But Okonkwo is a man characterized
by the rigidity of the weak: "his whole life was domi-

nated by fear, the fear of failure and of weakness"
(p. 10). He is perhaps the man in his clan most in need
of real freedom, and it is precisely psychological liberation which is denied him, partly because of his own
character and partly owing to the limited choice of life-
styles his society offers its members. He is, in other
words, the man who would have benefited the most from
Ikemefuna's continuing to live. The love he feels for
Ikemefuna, for his daughter Ezinma, and for Nwoye
when he responds to Ikemefuna's influence, Okonkwo is
afraid to admit or display: He "never showed any emotion openly, unless it be the emotion of anger. To show
affection was a sign of weakness; the only thing worth
demonstrating was strength" (p. 24).

Ikemefuna brings Okonkwo's potential for love almost
to the surface; after the boy's death Okonkwo shows
something like the grief born of love, but does not speak
of it. He is a man of action, continually unable to express much of his true self in words; ultimately he seems
to forget about the boy. Clearly Achebe is saying here
that Okonkwo is basically a good man. He can see
worth, if only certain kinds. But because of his lack of
truly free choice (not to be confused with free-will,
which he certainly has), he dares not acknowledge his
appreciation and his love. In a congenial setting with
more individual freedom, Okonkwo would probably accept at least the essentials of Christianity, as he accepts
its forerunner Ikemefuna. In this setting he wants only
to smash the alien religion. Like Ikemefuna, Okonkwo
comes along at the wrong time in the clan's history.

Furthermore, Okonkwo's killing of this Christ-figure
is integrally related to two of his other killings. Okonkwo is, to an even greater extent than his clan, an op-
poser and slayer of Youth. (Wise old Ezeudu and the
respected Obierika very strongly disapprove of Okonkwo's eagerness to participate in Ikemefuna's sacrifice

[pp. 49, 58–59].) Okonkwo administers th. *coup de grâce* to Ikemefuna; he accidentally kills Ezeudu's young son; and he morally and psychologically murders Nwoye. Even earlier, he keeps his children and his wives, "especially the youngest," perpetually frightened of him (p. 10). Only Ezinma and Ikemefuna please him, but Okonkwo manages to conceal even that; they too get their share of abuse (e.g., pp. 28, 39).

But, it may be objected, Okonkwo does become enthusiastic about some youngsters. Generally incapable of praising his own children, he does laud others': Obierika's son Maduka for his wrestling prowess and a young bridegroom for his skill at palm-tree tapping (pp. 57, 63). Such praise only apparently contradicts my assertion that Okonkwo is hostile to Youth. The deeds for which he admires these youngsters are specifically men's activities, the kind for which Okonkwo himself was once widely known. His praise of these young men is also wishful and wistful thinking. Nwoye because of his temperament, Ezinma because of her sex—and Ikemefuna because of his death—can never do these things that mean so much to Okonkwo.

All he really does in praising the young men is to praise his own early self. So long as people conform to his narrow standards they are acceptable to him; once they deviate even slightly he condemns them ruthlessly. Okonkwo detests Nwoye because the boy is too "womanish"; the same qualities in Ezinma would have been cherished. Even Ezinma is a disappointment to him though, for she is not a boy. He appreciates her only to the extent that she resembles him and is manly. Were Okonkwo less rigid, he could appreciate and love both his children for the individual human beings they are. "My children do not resemble me," he laments to Obierika after praising Maduka; "Where are the young suckers that will grow when the old banana tree dies?"

[63]

(pp. 57–58). Still earlier, in appealing to Nwakibie for yams with which to start his farm, Okonkwo has even more directly and consciously lauded himself. He tells Nwakibie of his willingness to work hard, stating: "The lizard that jumped from the high iroko tree to the ground said that he would praise himself if no one else did" (p. 18). The world will never be right enough for a man like Okonkwo. Ikemefuna, who might have been a mediator, is dead, and no one and nothing else comes up to Okonkwo's unrealistic standards.

As for Nwoye, it is no accidental choice of white man's names that Achebe has him make after his conversion; he is thenceforth called Isaac (p. 163). Abraham's sad willingness to sacrifice his beloved son is always regarded by Christian typology as looking forward to the Lord's sacrifice of His Son. Only for the Abraham of Umuofia there is no convenient angel to stay his hand. Achebe may well be saying that the original Abraham paid far too lightly for his crime against his own flesh and blood. Or perhaps Okonkwo is punished more heavily than his biblical prototype because, unlike the reluctant Abraham, he goes beyond what his religion demands. Here and elsewhere Achebe implicitly equates Okonkwo's world with the world of the Old Testament, with its narrowness and its violence, its emphasis on fear and on letter-of-the-law justice. He holds it up for us to compare unfavorably with "the new dispensation," with its love and mercy and flexibility, prefigured by Ikemefuna, brought by missionaries, and adopted by Nwoye.

The relationship between Nwoye and Ikemefuna now becomes clearer: they are literary doubles, dual aspects of a single son-figure. Okonkwo, in physically killing Ikemefuna, symbolically (and ironically) kills at the same time all that he considers manly in his own son. With Ikemefuna's coming, Nwoye had begun to change along the lines Okonkwo favored (pp. 45-47); and with

[64]

Ikemefuna's death, "something seemed to give way inside (Nwoye), like the snapping of a tightened bow" (p. 53). From this point onward Nwoye grows further and further away from Okonkwo, until he ultimately becomes a Christian and is disowned by him. Even earlier, in less obviously troubled times, Achebe carefully shows that an essential barrier has separated Okonkwo from Youth and Change. Ikemefuna, who is a forerunner of Christianity, and Nwoye, who becomes a Christian, are symbolically separated from Okonkwo. Engaged in covering the compound walls with palm branches and leaves, "Okonkwo worked on the outside of the wall and the boys worked from within" (p. 47, and emphasized again on p. 56). They are working at this task when the locusts, which are one of the key Christian symbols in the novel (as I show in another study), arrive in the village. At Okonkwo's death he is still "outside of the wall" (p. 184), cut off not only from his own ancestral spirits but from the new religion that might have allowed him to be a gentler person—a better son, husband, father, and clan-member.

Caesar Crosses the Niger

SHAKESPEARE AND ONITSHA MARKET CHAPBOOKS

by GENE ULANSKY

Comrades, Mpolo, Okito and the rest lend me your ears, for it is now that I am going to issue directives which will guide you until the war of liberation comes to an end. . . . This country is ours! We must not let it down! Belgium must pack away. . . .

Thus speaks Patrice Lumumba in *The Last Days of Lumumba,* a melange of fact and fancy spliced by quaint dialogue. Though a far cry from *Julius Caesar,* its snippets of political intrigue, Elizabethan flamboyance, and Shakespearean plot—typical of many pam-

[66]

phlets published in and around Onitsha, West Africa's largest market city and the center of its pamphlet trade —give it an engaging bicultural flavor.

By randomly dipping into the pamphlets one discovers that Onitsha market authors are ingenious in their efforts to satisfy readers, indifferent to accusations of plagiarism, and more eclectic than erudite. Their hundreds of available pamphlets offer sage advice (*How to Know Proverbs and Many Things, How to Avoid Poverty*), or promise entertaining stories of love (*Rosemary and the Taxi Driver, Disaster in the Realms of Love*), morality (*Money Hard to Get but Easy to Spend, Why Harlots Hate Married Men and Love Bachelors*) and power (*The Life Story and Death of John Kennedy, How Lumumba Suffered in Life and Died in Katanga, How Tshombe and Mobutu Regretted after the Death of Mr. Lumumba*).

Pamphlets written before 1966, Nigeria's year of assassination, genocide, and disintegration, are often prophetic and far closer to the facts of African life than government pronouncements and the uncritical eulogies which once appeared frequently in both African and Western presses. Many pamphlets add African flesh to Shakespearean bones; and when billowy Nigerian robes replace togas, Julius Caesar seems written for Africa, as Julius Nyerere, Tanzania's president, knew when he translated it into Swahili. Some—Thomas Iguh's playlets, for example—model their plots on *Julius Caesar* and add Shakespearean garnish to styles already strange and flamboyant.

In Iguh's *The Last Days of Lumumba,* the Counsel for Lumumba and his co-defendants urges the judge to discharge them "for they are as clean as the ostrich." In A. N. Mbah's *The Life Story of Zik,* a biography of Nigeria's ex-president, Nnamdi Azikiwe, one reads that Zik's father by taking a second wife "had asked for what

[67]

Mr. John Foster Dulles has aptly described as 'massive retaliation.' "

Given the volatility of African politics, Nigerian and Congolese in particular, it is no surprise to encounter variations of *Julius Caesar's* conspiracy scene. Iguh's *Dr. Zik in the Battle for Freedom* and *The Last Days of Lumumba* begin with secret meetings. Before Lumumba's address incites his followers to riot, he and his comrades gather to buoy one another.

MR. EVERISTUS

. . . I am prepared to die now, for it is better for one to die for the cause of his nation than dying in the glory of sleep.

MR. GIZENGA

Our policy from now should be positive action.

MR. OKITA

Was it not Winston Churchill who said, 'It is sweeter and more honourable to die in the battle field than in bed'?

MR. MPOLO

For myself, it is a question of giving me complete liberty or I take death!

PATRICE LUMUMBA

Are you all here with me prepared to execute any order I dish out to you?

MR. EVERISTUS

It is where you die that I must die too, Monsieur Lumumba.

MR. OKITA

I know that this great battle in front of us will be a bloody one, but let no one develop cold feet. . . .

[68]

Transplanted to Africa, the Roman forum becomes the market square, where Lumumba addresses his countrymen.

My dear country men, it gives me much pleasure to see all of you gathered here today for the cause of our dear Congo. We are not wood but men, and as such, it will be the height of our foolishness and stupidity to continue to swallow the atrocities which these hunger-stricken Belgians commit against our motherland. . . . We have paid taxes and rates only to see it sent over to Brussels for the development of the King's palace. What a rubbish and what a dirty record!

The hero of Iguh's *The Struggle and Trial of Jomo Kenyatta* is more mellow:

My dear country men and women. I am very pleased to be here with you today for it is a day of great mourning. Let me not take you astray for if I begin to recount what happened within the past days you and myself will shed tears.

Spirits far friendlier than Caesar's ghost enliven Iguh's playlets. The heroes, god-like themselves—women hold out their infants for Jomo Kenyatta's blessing—find nothing extraordinary about hobnobbing with divinity. In *Dr. Zik in the Battle for Freedom*, Zik nonchalantly converses with a spirit.

ZIK

Hello my lord—what is wrong again?

SPIRIT

Now listen: The sum of £10,000 has been paid to your driver by the Governor . . . to shoot

you. . . . So immediately I leave you now stop
him, search him, take the revulver [sic] from
him and pay him off on the spot. God doesn't
want anything to harm you until your life's mission's fulfilled. Bye-Bye.

On another occasion, while Zik is rousing a vast
throng with verbal fireworks, a spirit swoops down and
hands him a copy of a confidential letter written by Nigeria's British governor, stating his plan to start an anti-
Zik, anti-independence party. Zik muses momentarily,
then resumes.

Yes, good countrymen, I was talking to you
about the importance of positive action when an
Angel of the Lord came down and handed over
this document that I won't want you to know
what the contents are, for if I do so, it will stir
you to rage and mutiny. Governor Williams is
up against me with all his plans but I am now
going to tell him that if care is not taken the
blood of tyrants of his type must water the tree
of Nigerian freedom.

Patrice Lumumba also receives a visit from a spirit.

SPIRIT

In less than five minutes from now, your opponents will come to arrest you. But they will be
kept out of your house by the U.N. Ghanaian
Troops. . . . So you must be prepared to es-
cape. . . .

MRS. LUMUMBA

With whom were you talking dear?

PATRICE LUMUMBA

I have just received a message from God.

Heroes, by invoking Shakespearean language, cloak themselves with unimpeachable dignity. In *The Last Days of Lumumba,* as Tshombe slaps his captive around a prison cell, Lumumba, battered but self-possessed, comments, "I will never ask you to be merciful on me. What I would care to inform you is that the evil men do lives after them." His comrade Mpolo also suffers from Tshombe's blows. To Tshombe's "I am going to make you die the most ignominious death ever known!" Mpolo retorts, "The evil that men do lives after them! You want to reap where you didn't sow!"

Although Lumumba's counsel concludes his defense with a Shakespearean flourish,

> The Quality of Mercy is not Strained.
> It droppeth as the Gentle rain from
> Heaven,
> It Blessed Him that gives
> And Him that takes . . . ,

Portia's plea won't win an acquittal, for the genius of Congolese, Nigerian, and much of African politics is better captured by the conspiracy, assassination, demagoguery, and purges of *Julius Caesar,* as Onitsha market authors, their public and Africans far beyond the Niger know only too well.

Four Ghanaian Novels

by ROBERT E. McDOWELL

Potential readers of African novels in English (and particularly Americans), while watching for some political calm to descend over the vast African continent, have been largely oblivious to the literary maturity of Africa's young writers, in spite of the fact that African literary growth has far outstripped most other developments in modern African life. Thanks largely to British (and some African) publishers, western readers have come to know a few of the more important black writers from several countries: Chinua Achebe, Cyprian Ekwensi, and Amos Tutuola from Nigeria; James Ngugi from Kenya; Peter Abrahams and Alex La Guma from South Africa.

And now, equally provocative as books by these writers are three recent novels out of Ghana: J. W. Abru-

quah's *The Catechist* (George Allen & Unwin, 1965),
Francis Selormey's *The Narrow Path* (Heinemann, 1966),
and S. A. Konadu's *A Woman in Her Prime* (Heinemann, 1967). They illustrate not only "the slow, placid
prose of West Africa" (to borrow a phrase from Lewis
Nkosi) but also some of the primary themes of West
African writing. These are by no means the majority of
Ghanaian fiction writers, but they are of great importance as novel writers.[1]

The first two of these novels, like South African fiction, have been written close to the authors' own experiences. Abruquah certifies in his "Preface" that

> This book is based on a framework of reality
> —my father's life. Much of the detail, but not all
> of it, is fiction. Where real names are indispens-
> able, they are used. But the family represented
> here is all mixed up and renamed, with fresh
> characters assigned to different members.

Candid in its revelation, *The Catechist* is almost em-
barrassingly intimate at times because of its first-person
narration. Essentially, it is the late nineteenth and early
twentieth century annal of Afram, who should by
rights have been a Christian preacher, but who remained a lowly catechist, shuffled around mercilessly
to many run-down churches in remote communities, always moving, and while rearing his sons as educated
men, failing himself to gain a dignified position in life:

> I went. Always on the move. I was only a few
> months at Bobikuma; a year at the next Station,
> and so on until I was transferred farther and far-
> ther from home again. At most Stations I re-

[1] One can always make a fairly quantitative case for the novel, simply because of its ability to tell "the whole story" in a way the
short story cannot. This, naturally, does not dismiss the significance
of Ghana's better short story artists: Christiana A. Aidoo, Kwabena
Annan, Ellis Komey, Peter Kwame Buahin, and others.

placed inefficient Ministers who had ruined the mission house, estranged their congregations and neglected their duty. . . .

Thus the author narrates through the simple rhythms of the father, "the chief actor himself." It is indeed a fitting narration, for it is people of this catechist's era who felt most powerfully the bewildering rush of European ways, and it is to him and his contemporaries that history bequeathed the difficult task of spanning two cultures—the life of the rural African village and that of Europe-oriented Christianity. Clearly Afram exists between the two worlds:

> I was a Christian who still held tenaciously to the ancestral beliefs of my people.

Always the catechist feels the new system of which he is an active part pushing him, and more especially his sons, away from tradition:

> My own son now tells me my ideas are utter rubbish.

The congregations to which he ministers are no less a trial:

> On Sundays I conducted service in a little Wesleyan Chapel and preached to a congregation just emerging from paganism, myself a near pagan. I don't think Christianity meant more to those people or to me than a mere substitute for the witch-doctor.

When finally, aged and broken, Afram goes into retirement, he is understandably bitter about his career:

> I went quietly into obscurity with no laurels and no respect; no last-minute farewells or godspeeds; no visible means of support save that which my own sons were hopefully expected to give. For

> Catechists are the scum of the earth and com-
> mand no respect and expect none. They are en-
> titled to no gratuities or pension and when they
> are strong enough to outlive their usefulness . . .
> "God will provide."

Beyond doubt, the core of this novel has to do with estrangement: with Afram's constant dwelling among strange people with strange ways; with his separation from those close to him. Brought up as a boy in a wholly African environment, Afram seems much of the time to be unconscious of the potential for change in the alien Christian beliefs which he disperses to his fellows. But, of course, how can he *in medias res* know the new ways that must necessarily open up after the European invasion of African minds. It is ironic that Afram's greatest pride is in the education of his sons:

> My own personal failures were as nothing com-
> pared with the achievements of my sons.

The rapid move away from the spirit presences of the Fante, the swift turn toward the technological twentieth century life—in short, the move from all that Afram felt most comfortable in, is manifest in these educated young Ghanaian men.

Francis Selormey's novel is strikingly similar to Abru-quah's. Once more the story is biographical and is in large part the story of the father, Nani. Like Afram, Nani is a Christian, a Catholic who translates for the white priests, directs the church choir, and performs as headmaster of a primary school. In this novel the son, Kofi, narrates. He describes himself (born in the 1920's) as caught between traditional African modes and Christian ones: he is born in a French hospital at Lome, but cured of his first illness by a witch doctor. A little later his sister Ami has both the traditional and a Catholic baptism:

A strong drink called "Akpeteshi"—was poured out, that the unfriendly spirits might drink it and become drunk and so forget any evil designs they might have had on the child.

. . . . .

In the afternoon, Ami was baptized in the Catholic Church and given a Christian name.

This family, like Afram's, is constantly forced by the church to move. With each new school Nani takes over, Kofi feels that he is treated as an example for the rest of the pupils. The father is indeed often overly severe. Once, for instance, he hangs Kofi up by bound wrists, beats him as he hangs on a wall, takes him to the classroom and gives him twenty-five more strokes with a cane, then kicks him in the side. Not surprisingly, the child is unable to rise from his bed for a week.

But not all is horrible in *The Narrow Path*. There are pleasant episodes such as Kofi's relationship with a kindly teacher and scout leader, and his fruitful years with the family of his "master." Yet throughout the story, family difficulties build up until events seem to scream out at us. Nani is transferred by the church again and again, always to more primitive areas with poor schools and few Christians. In one community there is a murder by witchcraft. With the expense of the children's schooling and the necessity over and again of constructing new housing, the family breaks apart. The mother goes to her people and Nani stubbornly keeps the children and goes to live with his family near his new school. As with Afram's sons, Kofi, at the end, is going off for a higher education:

The college was 200 miles away, and it seemed to my mother that I was going to the end of the earth. We all rose at dawn on the day of my leaving. My mother filled a calabash with water and sprinkled corn-dough into it. She raised it to the east and to the west, and she invoked all the family gods, and asked that they would protect me on my journey, guard and guide me. . . .

Clearly, Selormey's is a story of disintegration, experienced not just once, but many times. Every move was a nightmare to the family:

Ho was an inland town, eighty-six miles away. None of us, except my father, had ever travelled so far. We were to leave our family and friends, to leave the sea and the shore, the lagoon and the coconut trees, and the fresh fish that formed the most valuable part of our diet. We felt lost and bewildered. People said that the customs of the Ho people were different from our own. . . .

The change of worlds over a short span of time has been made to appear vast. Kofi's grandfather had had eight wives; his son had gone into a strange religion called Catholicism; the grandson, Kofi, becomes a college graduate, and much less conservative than his father. In the end, the larger family relationship is in shambles for Nani. He and his wife have experienced a terrible breach; there grows an ever greater rift between him and his son Kofi; and Kofi's cousins all label him as conceited because of his book learning. Without knowing, Nani has, like Afram, participated in a bewildering cultural transition; he has been very much part of a European-instigated revolution.

The closeness of Abruquah's and Selormey's works to many Nigerian novels is often great, as one would expect from writers whose nations have shared similar colonial experiences. Perhaps most evident here is the sort of thing one reads about in Chinua Achebe's novels —the breakdown of the communal code in African life, and the subsequent vulnerability of Africans to European individualism. Is there here the feeling of a whole civilization having been slowly dissolved. When colonial administrators and churchmen force drastic changes in the patterns of an essentially rural African life, all social loyalties are necessarily shaken at their roots.

Quite different from these two novels, but equally involved in telling the story of Ghanaians, is Konadu's short novel, *A Woman in Her Prime*. It is a lyrical description of a simple people, untouched by Europe, villagers caught up completely in animist ritual, a group very much at the mercy of the elements, people still called together by the crier pounding a gong. *A Woman in Her Prime* is an interesting foil for the other two books: while they are powerfully disintegrative, this annal shows essentially the coherence of traditional village life. And though the heroine undergoes many trials throughout the story, her life seems to come to a natural and satisfactory full circle in the end.

The woman in her prime, Pokuwaa, has tragically failed to conceive. This attractive woman and successful farmer has divorced her first two husbands, believing them to be incapable of giving her a child. With the third marriage there is again reason to believe that her partner is at fault. Perhaps because he has another wife, Kwadwo spends most of his time sleeping when he is around Pokuwaa. From the community, however, Pokuwaa has plenty of encouragement to bear a child. Her mother, as indeed the entire village, seems to inject prayers for fertility into most of their chants:

Let all who are barren bear children.
Let all who are impotent find remedy.

But such supplications appear more and more futile to Pokuwaa, and so she finally declares to Kwadwo:

I will not go on with the sacrifices.

. . . . .

"I am a woman," said Pokuwaa. "And a woman
does want a child; that is her nature. But if a
child will not come, what can I do? I can't spend
my whole life bathing in herbs."

Pokuwaa's old mother expresses the dismay of the whole
village over her daughter's plight:

What is the fate of a state destined to be if its
women refuse to give birth? Where are the sons
who will defend the land going to come from?

When at last Pokuwaa does conceive, there is nearly
delirious joy in her family, and a celebration of sorts in
the village:

Under the village silk cotton tree, many cala-
bashes of palm wine passed round amidst male
jokes aimed at the man who was expecting a
child with such unrivalled pride. If the heavy
rains had not let themselves down, and broken up
the daily party, the men would have been pleased
to continue using Kwadwo to justify long drink-
ing bouts.

As for Pokuwaa,

The rain could not dampen her spirits. Her
mother, Koramoa and Kwadwo were around her;
her child inside her, kicking.

Whether or not the conception proves that supplications to the Great God Tano have been noticed, everyone in the community besides Pokuwaa believes it. At
any rate, Pokuwaa, now at a fairly advanced age for
child bearing, achieves fulfillment at the end of the
story. Here are problems which work themselves out in
the ordinary course of events in the milieu of the traditional Ghanaian village. The heroine, often at odds with

[79]

herself as well as with her immediate family, is nevertheless a character who despite a time of great despair, never flagrantly abandons time-honored modes. She is never seen as an outsider; she remains essentially an integral part of her village.

The history of the revision of Ghanaian life as seen through the characters of Abruquah and Selormey is provocative. But this sort of movement and change is not, as Konadu shows us through his work, the only possibility for the Ghanaian novel. *A Woman in Her Prime* exhibits the sort of existence which preceded the dissolution recorded in Abruquah's and Selormey's works. It is a fascinating picture of people absolutely free from European inhibitions. Certainly it proves once more what a rich mine of material West African writers have at hand. Konadu's novelette suggests something of the natural joy we feel in Nwankwo's *Danda,* while at the same time something of the compelling fascination of animism so powerfully rendered in the several short books of Amos Tutuola. Whatever else these recent novels from Ghana tell us, they prove once again the ability of African novelists to directly confront the diversity and complexity of African experiences and intelligently interpret them for the world.

POETRY

For Biafra

by OBIAGELI PETERS

They say no tree can make a forest,
But what forest can survive
If treewitched and branched out of existence?
We bleed we bleed,
Each drop a sacrificial life sap.

They say no man is an island.
But what island can stand
A turbulent sea that greedily
Eats up its jutting sides
Ever slicing ever pressing?

They say man cannot live by bread alone.
Israel got its manna by turning
Its umbrella upside down.

[83]

Whoever heard of death by hunger
When there is promise of release?

We bleed we bleed,
We must atone for our lost seed.

Dogged and rugged
I take my stand.
I dig my astride feet into the earth,
I am turned to molten.
For the deer swallowed the deer to live,
Only he could not leave.
The child playing with his chewing gum
Did not know the gum does not know when.

We bleed we bleed,
We must atone for our lost seed.

The ass lets everything pass.
It has had its hour it said,
One long and sweet.
Burdened and tired I must ask for mine.
For having swallowed me,
You cannot be free.

They say the closest thing to death is sleep.
We took a nap and bid our time
Our enemy thought we were dead,
But they forget there is only one resurrection
And whatever follows is an insurrection.

We bleed we bleed
We must atone for our lost seed.
We heard the echo before the voice,
And we have no choice.

[84]

Mélancolie et Rêverie
TWELVE POEMS

by JEAN IKELLE-MATIBA [1]

Berlin

Ville-parade
tes rues rappellent les pompes anciennes
ville-verdure
les lacs les bois les forêts t'entourent
d'une ceinture verdoyante
des parcs des jardins
guirlande naturelle que tressent les saisons
te servent de parure

L'angoisse
  l'incertitude
    voilà tes compagnes

les promenades

[1] See also pages 211 to 213.

les cafés aussi
et les salles de concert
tes lieux de rendez-vous

Les lettres et les arts
la liberté crèatrice
ta couronne

Le poète et l'artiste tes nouveaux souverains
refont à leur manière l'étiquette prussienne

    Berlin
  Unter den Linden
    Berlin
  Alexanderplatz
    Berlin
  Kurfürstendamm
    Berlin
  Tempelhof

  Place d'Empire
  Voici Bismarck guindé
  Moltke rêveur
  Roon solennel
  La Berolina pleure sur sa ville détruite

Le Reichtag vers le ciel dresse son masque opaque
la porte de Brandenburg est maintenant encerclée
les dômes éventrés offrent un visage meurtri
à côté des ruines grandioses surgissent des église neuves

  Vive le ciel bleu
    un avion bourdonne au-dessus de la ville
    le bruit des klaxons viole mon silence:
    un lointain monarque en visite officielle

[86]

Leipzig

Une musique langoureuse invite les danseurs
Des couples dans la piste doucement se caressent
Leipzig est toujours là comme au temps de Goethe
avec sa poésie sa musique et son rythme

Le monument des Nations se dresse à l'horizon
Et rappelle au touriste Dix-huit-cent-treize
Dans son immensité le musée Dimitroff engloutit son
   héros
L'hôtel municipal évoque le Moyen Age
malgré ses lampes rouges brillant en permanence

L'Eglise Saint-Thomas avec ses choeurs d'enfants
et la tombe du Grand Bach ne s'oublie jamais

Revoir Leipzig est toujours un plaisir

Souvenir d'Italie

Sous la griserie du vin de Toscane
nous dormions en silence

Doucement
tout doucement
tu pris ta mandoline
et jouas une chanson du midi
o la voluptueuse musique napolitaine

Lointaine est l'Italie
avec ses orangers
son ciel toujours bleu
Et ses éternelles vacances

L'air d'alors me revient souvent
il contenait un message d'amour d'espoir d'éternité

A l'Inconnu

Tu chercheras ma soeur
une place vide devant toi
tu chercheras mon frère
il ne sera plus là
tu appelleras ma mère
seul l'écho répondra
tu voudras revoir mon père
on te montrera une tombe

Et tu seras ému
à quoi sert ton chagrin

Les morts se sont tus
la mort a fermé leur bouche
bouché leurs oreilles
raidi leurs membres
clos leurs paupières
Le soleil s'est caché
les lucioles éteintes
la lune ne brille plus
maintenant le nuit noire

Agis
pour que du néant sorte un renouveau
travaille
redresse les ruines
rebâtis la cité
afin que d'autres aient la vie plus clémente

Là-bas

dans la pénombre
joue une meute d'enfants
éclaire leur jour
assure leur avenir
toi l'unique espoir

Agir
voilà ton lot

Sous le froid

Sur le pont
du bateau
j'ai attendu
malgré la nuit
malgré le vent

Le bateau parti
le phare s'est éteint

Sur le quai
tremblant de froid
en vain
en vain
j'ai attendu

Une Nuit d'orage

La nuit
m'entoure
Et
j'ai peur
du vent
qui hurle
sans cesse

La vent
sans cesse
hurle
sous ma fenêtre
Et
j'entends
le fracas
des éclairs

Les éclairs
déchirent
le ciel
tourmenté

Les nuages
gouttent
Partout
de l'eau

Et
le matin
les arbres arrachés
jonchent le sol

Le Nord

J'ai désiré la brume
les nuits enveloppées de brouillard
du nord
les tristes soirées monotones
les regards mélancoliques
la solitude

J'ai voulu fuir le sud
son rythme

[90]

sa gaité naturelle
son climat fascinant
Le nord m'attire

J'ai voulu écouter la musique nostalgique
les jours d'hiver
vivre avec mon double afin de me connaître
le nord m'attirait

J'y ai laissé mon âme

Le Printemps

Le moineau chante
l'hirondelle
rejoint son nid

voici
les fleurs
le printemps est là

La vie
lentement
reprend son souffle
la neige fond
tout
se renouvelle

Voici
le printemps
parmi nous

Intégration

Des fleurs
toutes blanches
je t'ai offert
des roses
des roses de chez moi

Tu n'en croyais pas tes jeux
et pensais sans doute
qu'elles venaient de chez toi

J'ai vu des arbres verts
comme je les vois chez moi

Des ruisseaux limpides
des fleuves au courant sauvage
comme chez moi

J'ai vu la plaine immense
la montagne imprenable
comme je les vois chez moi

J'ai vu des hommes heureux
au délicieux sourire
des hommes tristes hagards éperdus
comme chez moi

Les oiseaux ici chantent comme chez nous
les animaux l'été tondent le pré
comme ils le font chez nous

Des amoureux
l'air heureux
sont venus vers moi

Amie
quelle est ta différence?

[92]

Mélancolie

Il pleut
de l'eau
du gris
Pleure mon coeur
le sanglot
erraille ma gorge
Tristesse

Hier
le vent
le soleil
les bourrasques
les feuilles
Aujourd'hui
la pluie
le silence
le froid
Nuit

Jeunesse
bel âge
solitude
travail
Et après
la récolte
du monde
Destin

De ce pays
autrefois
peuplé et prospère
je rentre
Partout désolation
ennui

O temps
arréte ta faux
afin que nous puissions
redresser les ruines

Des cris
des pleurs
je ne veux plus entendre

Vivement le ciel bleu
le soleil
la gaité
La Joie

Autrefois

Le vent
qui murmure
m'apporte un message
d'amour

Tendresse et beauté
espoir et jeunesse
me faisaient vivre
alors

Le silence studieux
du créateur pensif
est devenue mon lot

Et
je me rappelle
parfois
le vent murmurant

[94]

son message
d'amour

Rêverie

Un ciel bas
des arbres effeuillés
une nature triste
un horizon maussade
L'univers où gravite mon âme
et je me sens triste
triste et las
las des voyages sans fin

Et mon esprit s'envole vers le passé
passé désormais éteint
mais qui me fait vivre à mesure que je vieillis

J'entends encore des chants
les chants des piroguiers
J'entends leurs pagaies fendre le fleuve
je vois les rivages sombres de la Sanaga
Ce fut un temps heureux

Mais c'est l'hiver sans neige
les cours boueuses
les routes verglassées
Ils descendent par milliers
dans des voitures encombrées
les promeneurs de dimanche
ils se racontent des histoires en rongeant leur
frein
sifflent crient gesticulent
et se croient heureux

Les piroguiers sont morts
le fleuve devenu désert
nul n'entendra plus l'écho de leurs voix

Alors le dimanche nous n'aurons plus des rameurs
mais des hors-bord au bruit assourdissant
des jeunes femmes aux seins enveloppés
et nous rirons ensemble
ensemble sur les bancs de sable
nous prendrons des bains de soleil

    Un vent timide anime les arbres
    le clocher devant moi prend l'air désolé
    le gazon pousse lentement
    par moment chantent les oiseaux
    triste chant rappelant la nuit

Où coule la Sanaga telle que je la connus
où sont ses piroguiers
Dis, voyageur, et les arbres qui se moquaient de saison

    Dans un parc immense
    par des allées mouillées
    je me promène solitaire
    écoutant siffler la brise
    qui rappelle un vent d'automne

    Au mur pend
    un portrait de mes vingt ans
    heureux âge qui ne s'oublie jamais

    Oui
    il faudra ranimer la cendre
    rendre à la Sanaga ses chanteurs et son charme
    lui redonner un coeur
    une âme

reviendront les piroguiers
mais d'un nouvel âge

Le dimanche
la prière
et après
comme autrefois la baignade
les cris joyeux d'enfants
espoir du lendemain

Et coule toujours la Sanaga
confiante

Ten Poems

by DAVID DIOP [1]

A ma mère

Quand autour de moi surgissent les souvenirs
Souvenirs d'escales anxieuses au bord du gouffre
De mers glacés où se noient les moissons
Quand revivent en moi les jours à la dérive
Les jours en lambeaux à goût de narcotique
Où derrière les volets clos
Le mot se fait aristocrate pour enlacer le vide
Alors mère je pense à toi
A tes belles paupières brûlées par les années
A ton sourire sur mes nuits d'hôpital
Ton sourire qui disait les vieilles misères vaincues
O mère mienne et qui est celle de tous
Du nègre q'on aveugla et qui revoit les fleurs
Ecoute écoute ta voix
Elle est ce cri traversé de violence
Elle est ce chant guidé seul par l'amour.

---

[1] The poems were selected from *Coups de Pilon* (Paris: *Présence Africaine*, 1961). English translations by Paulette J. Trout and Ellen Conroy Kennedy.

For My Mother

When all about me memories arise
Memories of anxious hangings on the edge of cliffs
Of icy seas where harvests drown
When drifting days come back to me
Ragged days with a narcotic taste
When the word becomes aristocrat
To overcome the emptiness
Behind closed blinds
Then mother I think of you
Of your beautiful eyelids burnt by the years
Of your smile on my hospital nights
Your smile that told of old and vanquished miseries
O mother mine mother of us all
Of the Negro they blinded who once again sees flowers
Listen listen to your voice
This cry shot through with violence
This song that springs only from love.

Les Vautours

En ce temps-là
A coups de gueule de civilisation
A coups d'eau bénite sur les fronts domestiqués
Les vautours construisaient à l'ombre de leurs serres
Le sanglant monument de l'ère tutélaire
En ce temps-là
Les rires agonisaient dans l'enfer métallique des routes
Et le rythme monotone des Pater-Nosters
Couvrait les hurlements des plantations à profit
O le souvenir acide des baisers arrachés
Les promesses mutilées au choc des mitrailleuses
Hommes étranges qui n'étiez pas des hommes
Vous saviez tous les livres vous ne saziez pas l'amour
Et les mains qui fécondent le ventre de la terre
Les racines de nos mains profondes comme la révolte
Malgré vos chants d'orgueil au milieu des charniers
Les villages désolés l'Afrique écartelée
L'espoir vivait en nous comme une citadelle
Et des mines du Souaziland à la sueur lourde des usines
   d'Europe
Le printemps prendra chair sous nos pas de clarté.

The Vultures

There once was a time
When with civilization's ugly blows
With the spread of holy water upon domesticated brows
The vultures built in the shadows of their claws
The bleeding monuments to their tutelary era

There once was a time
When laughter was drowned in the metallic hell of roads
And the monotonous rhythm of *Pater-Nosters*
Covered the screams that rose from the plantations

O the acid memory of torn embraces
Promises mutilated by machine-gun fire

Strange men
You were not men
You knew all the books
You knew not love

While our hands made pregnant the belly of the earth
The roots of our hands went as deep as revolt

Despite your proud songs in the midst of your carnals
Desolated villages, Africa so shackled
Hope lived within us like a citadel
And from Swaziland's mines to Europe's sweat-filled
    factories
Springtime will be born beneath our light steps.

Les Heures

Il y a des heures pour rêver
Dans l'apaisement des nuits au creux du silence
Il y a des heures pour douter
Et le lourd voile des mots se déchire en sanglots
Il y a des heures pour souffir
Le long des chemins de guerre dans le regard des mères
Il y a des heures pour aimer
Dans les cases de lumière où chante la chair unique
Il y a ce qui colore les jours à venir
Comme le soleil colore la chair des plantes
Et dans le délire des heures
Dans l'impatience des heures
Le germe toujours plus fécond
Des heures d'où naîtra l'équilibre.

Times

There are times for dreaming
In the peacefulness of nights with hollow silences
And times for doubt
When the heavy web of words is torn with sighs
There are times for suffering
Along the roads of war at the look in mothers' eyes
There are times for love
In lighted huts where one flesh sings
There is what colours times to come
As sunshine greens the plants
In the delirium of these hours
In the impatience of these hours
Is the ever fertile seed
Of times when equilibrium is born

Auprès de toi

Auprès de toi j'ai retrouvé mon nom
Mon nom longtemps caché sous le sel des distances
J'ai retrouvé les yeux que ne voilent plus les fièvres
Et ton rire comme la flamme trouant l'ombre
M'a redonné l'Afrique au delà des neiges d'hier
Dix ans mon amour
Et les matins d'illusions et les débris d'idées
Et les sommeils peuplés d'alcool
Dix ans et le souffe du monde m'a versé sa souffrance
Cette souffrance qui charge le présent du goût des
    lendemains
Et fait de l'amour un fleuve sans mesure
Auprès de toi j'ai retrouvé la mémoire de mon sang
Et les colliers de rires autour des jours
Les jours qui étincellent de joies renouvelées.

With You

With you I have refound my name
My name long hidden neath the salt of distances
I have rediscovered eyes no longer fever-dimmed
And your laughter like a flame piercing the darkness
Once more has brought me Africa despite the snows of
    yesterday
Ten years my love
Mornings of illusion and the remnants of ideas
And sleep inhabited by alcohol
Ten years and the breathing of the world has poured its
    pain on me
This suffering that weights the present with tomorrow's
    taste
And makes of love a boundless river
With you I have refound the memory of my blood
And necklaces of laughter round my days
Days that sparkle with joys renewed.

Le Renégat

Mon frère aux dents qui brillent sous le compliment
   hypocrite
Mon frère aux lunettes d'or
Sur tes yeux rendus bleus par la parole du Maître
Mon pauvre frère au smoking à revers de soie
Piaillant et sussurant et plastronnant dans les salons de
   la condescendance
Tu nous fais pitié
Le soleil de ton pays n'est plus qu'une ombre
Sur ton front serein de civilisé
El la case de ta grand'mère
Fait rougir un visage blanchi par les années d'humiliation
   et de Mea Culpa
Mais lorsque repu de mots sonores et vides
Comme la caisse qui surmonte tes épaules
Tu fouleras la terre amère et rouge d'Afrique
Ces mots angoissés rythmeront alors ta marche inquiète
Je me sens seul si seul ici!

The Renegade

My brother with the teeth that gleam at hypocritical
 compliments
My brother with the gold-rimmed eyes that reflect the
 Master's blue ones
My poor brother in the silk-faced dinner jacket
Squealing murmuring and strutting in condescending
 drawing rooms
We pity you
The sunshine of your homeland is but a shadow now
On your brow serenely civilized
And your grandmother's hut
Would make a face turned white by years of humiliation
 and *mea culpa*
Blush
But when
Full of sonorous and empty words
Like the great drum that stands upon your shoulders
You tread the red and bitter earth of Africa
These anguished words will mark the beat of your uneasy
 steps
I feel alone, so lonely here!

Afrique

A MA MÈRE

Afrique mon Afrique
Afrique des fiers guerriers dans les savanes ancestrales
Afrique que chante ma grand'Mère
Au bord de son fleuve lointain
Je ne t'ai jamais connue
Mais mon regard est plein de ton sang
Ton beau sang noir à travers les champs répandu
Le sang de ta sueur
La sueur de ton travail
Le travail de l'esclavage
L'esclavage de tes enfants
Afrique dis-moi Afrique
Est-ce donc toi ce dos qui se courbe
Et se couche sous le poids de l'humilité
Ce dos tremblant à zébrures rouges
Qui dit oui au fouet sur les routes de midi
Alors gravement une voix me répondit
Fils impétueux cet arbre robuste et jeune.
Cet arbre là-bas
Splendidement seul au milieu de fleurs blanches et
    fanées
C'est l'Afrique ton Afrique qui repousse
Qui repousse patiemment obstinément
Et dont les fruits ont peu à peu
L'amère saveur de la liberté.

Africa

TO MY MOTHER

Africa my Africa
Africa of proud warriors in ancestral savannas
Africa my grandmother sings of on a distant riverbank
I have never known you
But my face is filled with your blood
Your beautiful black blood spread across the fields
The blood of your sweat
The sweat of your toils
The toils of your slavery
The slavery of your children
Africa tell me Africa
Is it yours this back that is bending
Bowed low by humility's weight
This trembling red zebra-striped back
Saying yes to the whip on the sweltering roads
Then gravely a voice answered me
Impetuous son this young and robust tree
This very tree
In splendid isolation
Amid the white and wilted flowers
Is Africa your Africa growing again
Patiently stubbornly rising again
And little by little whose fruit
Bears freedom's bitter flavour.

A un enfant noir

Quinze ans
Et la vie comme une promesse un royaume entrevu

Dans le pays où les maisons touchent le ciel
Mais où le cœur n'est pas touché
Dan le pays où l'on pose la main sur la Bible
Mais où la Bible n'est pas ouverte
La vie à quinze ans apaise la faim des fleuves
La vie des peaux d'enfer des nom-de-Dieu de nègres
L'enfant noir un soir d'août perpétra le crime
Il osa l'infâme se servir de ses yeux
Et son regard rêva sur une bouche sur des seins sur un
    corps de Blanche
Ce corps enfant noir que seul aux sex-parties
Le Blanc peut saccager au rythme de tes blues
(Le nègre quelquefois sous des murs anonymes)
Le crime ne paie pas te l'avait-on assez dit
Et pour que justice soit faite ils furent deux
Juste deux sur le plateau de la balance
Deux hommes sur tes quinze ans et le royaume entrevu
Ils pensèrent à l'aveugle fou qui voyait
Aux femmes éclaboussées
Au règne qui trébuchait
Et ta tête vola sous les rires hystériques.

Dans les villas climatisées
Autour des boissons fraîches
La bonne conscience savoure son repos.

For a Black Child

Life
At fifteen
Is a promise, a kingdom half-glimpsed

In the land where houses touch the sky
Although the heart remains untouched
Where hands are placed upon the Bible
Though the Bible is unopened
A fifteen-year-old life can allay the river's hunger
A no-count god-damned nigger life
A black boy on an August eve did perpetrate the crime
Did dare the infamy to use his eyes and glance
To speculate about a white
Mouth and breasts and body
A black boy that only whites at orgies can ravish
    to the rhythm of your blues
(the black man only sometimes in anonymous rooms)
Crime doesn't pay you'd oft been told
And so justice could be done there were two
Exactly two on the platform of the scale
Two men against your fifteen years and the kingdom
    half-glimpsed
They thought of the crazy old blind man who saw
Of their women besmirched
Of the order that was tottering
And your head flew off to the sound of hysterical laughter

In air-conditioned mansions
Over cool drinks
Good conscience gloats
In its tranquility

Rama Kam

Me plaît ton regard de fauve
Et ta bouche a la saveur de mangue
  Rama Kam
Ton corps est le piment noir
Qui fait chanter le désir
  Rama Kam
Quand tu passes
La plus belle est jalouse
Du rythme chaleureux de ta hanche
  Rama Kam
Quand tu danses
Le tam-tam Rama-Kam
Le tam-tam tendu comme un sexe de victoire
Halète sous les doigts bondissants du griot
Et quand tu aimes
Quand tu aimes Rama Kam
C'est la tornade qui tremble
Dans ta chair de nuit d'éclairs
Et me laisse plein du souffle de toi
  O Rama Kam!

Rama Kam

The wildness of your glances pleases me
Your mouth has the taste of mango
      Rama Kam
Your body is the black pimento
That makes desire sing
      Rama Kam
As you pass
The handsomest woman is made jealous
By the warm rhythm of your hips
      Rama Kam
As you dance
To the tom-tom Rama Kam
The tom-tom taut as my victorious sex
Throbs beneath the griot's leaping fingers
When you love me Rama Kam
A tornado shakes
In the fiery blackness of your flesh
And fills me with your breath
      O Rama Kam!

Nègre clochard

À AIMÉ CÉSAIRE

Toi qui marchais comme un vieux rêve brisé
Un rêve foudroyé sous les lames du mistral
Par quels chemins de sel
Par quels détours de boue de souffrance acceptée
Par quelles caravelles plantant d'îles en îles
Les drapeaux de sang nègre arrachés de Guinée
As-tu conduit ta défroque d'épines
Jusqu'au cimetière étrange où tu lisais le ciel
Je vois dans tes yeux les haltes courbées de désespoir
Et l'aube recommencant le coton et les mines
Je vois Soundiata l'oublié
Et Chaka l'indomptable
Enfouis au fond des mers avec les contes de soie et de feu
Je vois tout cela
Des musiques martiales claironnant l'appel au meurtre
Et des ventres qui s'ouvrent dans des paysages de neige
Pour rassurer la peur tapie au creux des villes
O mon vieux nègre moissonneur de terres inconnues
Terres odorantes où chacun pouvait vivre
Qu'ont-ils fait de l'aurore qui s'ouvrait sur ton front
De tes pierres lumineuses et de tes sabres d'or
Te voici nu dans ta prison fangeuse
Volcan éteint offert aux rires des autres
A la richesse des autres
A la faim hideuse des autres
Ils t'appelaient Blanchette c'était si pittoresque
Et ils secouaient leurs grandes gueules à principes
Heureux du joli mot pas méchants pour un sou
Mais moi moi qu'ai-je fait dans ton matin de vent et de
    larmes

Negro Tramp

FOR AIMÉ CÉSAIRE

You who walked like a broken old dream
Laid low by the mistral's blades
Along what salty paths
Along what detours muddy with suffering accepted
Aboard what caravels from isle to isle planting flags of
   Negro blood torn away from Guinea
Have you worn your cast-off cloak of thorns
To the foreign graveyard where you used to read the sky
In your eyes I see you halt, stooped and in despair
And dawns when cotton and the mines began again
I see Soundiata the forgotten
And the indomitable Chaka
Hidden neath the seas with the tales of silk and fire
All this I see
Martial music and the clarion call to murder
And bellies gaping open in snowy countrysides
To pacify the fear cowering in the cities
O my old Negro harvester of unknown lands
Sweet scented lands where everyone could live
What have they made of the dawn that used to open on
   your brow
Of your luminous stones and golden sabres
Look at you naked in your filthy prison
A dead volcano for others to laugh at
For others to get rich on
To feed their awful hunger
Whitey they called you how picturesque
Shaking their fat, high-principled heads
Pleased with their joke, not nasty at all
But I, what did I do on your windy weeping morning

Dans ce matin noyé d'écume
Où pourrissaient les couronnes sacrées
Qu'ai-je fait sinon supporter assis sur mes nuages
Les agonies nocturnes
Les blessures immuables
Les guenilles pétrifiées dan les camps d'épouvante
Le sable était de sang
Et je voyais le jour pareil aux autres jours
Et je chantais Yéba
Yéba à pleine folic les zoos en délire
O plantes enterrées
O semences perdues
Pardonne nègre mon guide
Pardonne mon cœur étroit
Les victoires retardées l'armure abandonnée
Patience le Carnaval est mort
J'aiguise l'ouragan pour les sillons futurs
Pour toi nous referons Ghâna et Tombouctou
Et les guitares peuplées de galops frénétiques
A grands coups de pilons sonores
De pilons
Eclatant
De case en case
Dans l'azur pressenti.

That morning drowned in seafoam
When the sacred cows decayed
What did I do seated on my clouds but tolerate
The nocturnal dyings
The immutable wounds
The petrified rags in the terror stricken camps
The sand seemed made of blood
And I saw a day like any other day
And I sang Yeba
Yeba like a raving animal
O buried plants
O lost seeds
Forgive me Negro guide
Forgive my narrow heart
The victories postponed the armour abandoned
Patience the Carnival is done
I am sharpening a hurricane to plough the future with
For you we shall remake Ghana and Timbuktu
And guitars will galop wildly
In great shuddering chords
Like the hammerblows of pestles
Pounding mortars
Bursting forth
From hut to hut
Into the portentive blue.

Le Temps du martyr

Le Blanc a tué mon père
Car mon père était fier
Le Blanc a violé ma mère
Car ma mère était belle
Le Blanc a courbé mon frère sous le soleil des routes
Car mon frère était fort
Puis le Blanc a tourné vers moi
Ses mains rouges de sang
       Noir
M'a craché son mépris au visage
Et de sa voix de maître:
"Hé boy, un Berger, une serviette, de l'eau!"

The Time of Martyraom

The White man killed my father
For my father was proud
The White man raped my mother
For my mother was beautiful
The White man bent my brother beneath the roadway
    sun
For my brother was strong
Then the White man turned to me
His hands red with Black blood
Spit his scorn in my face
And with his voice of Master called:
"Hey, Boy! Bring me a napkin and a drink!"

SHORT
STORIES

The Intruder

by P. W. SONGA [1]

Engaruka spread out before him like a shallow bowl.
Sitting on a crag on top of a dome-shaped hill, he was
like a fly sitting on a lump of food. Behind him was a
wall of mountains, to his left continued the plain, broken
only by the dark form of an extinct volcano some five
miles away, looking like a sleeping giant. Another chain
of mountains looking blue and hazy stood far ahead. Behind those distant ranges lay an unknown world. To
his right, the almost endless flatness vanished on the
horizon, shimmering as far as the eye could see, only
occasionally interrupted by a tree, or the neck of a
giraffe.

The basin was like a hot bath in the afternoon heat.
The air trembled with a brightness that dazed the on-

[1] Reprinted from *Darlite*, No. 1, University College, Dar es Salaam.

looker. Everything was harshly brown except for the fresh green strip of oasis describing the course of the river. Tumbling through a narrow gorge in the wall of mountains behind him, the river cut a straight course until it reached the lowest point of the plain, before it began winding its way in great loops into the glaring lake.

Mungo caught sight of two brown figures coming from the left, the direction of the river, carrying what looked like bundles of reeds. Each held his spear in his right hand while with the other he balanced his bundle on his head. Masai: he could not mistake them. They were probably carrying the reeds to the *manyatta* lying below the hill a little to the right. About a mile ahead, a column of dust hung in the air. He could see dark figures making their way to the glittering lake.

The two Masai were coming up the hill, having laid down their bundles, and now carried only their spears. He felt uneasy. What could be bringing them up here? He calmed himself and increased the volume of the transistor radio set beside him—they might get interested in the music. Presently, he could hear them panting behind him; he turned around and smiled at them. They smiled back, exposing their coppery teeth, and said cheerfully,

"Jambo, bwana!"

"Sijambo. 'Abari gani?" he ventured in his best Swahili.

Silence ensued. They regarded each other with curious smiles. Neither side seemed willing to take charge. He was as handicapped as they were, because he was new to the country, while they were not well-grounded in the "national" language. His eyes swept slowly across the plain and then turned to the mountains for a while. Then he looked back at the Masai; they were getting eager for conversation. This, their country, was fascinating; so different from those other parts he was familiar with. He broke the silence and pointed to the dark form of the volcanic mountain:

"That mountain, what is it called?"

"Ol Donyo . . . . ; and that one behind is Oldonyo l'Engai. That one where the sun rises is Oldonyo Sambu."

"Why is each of them an Oldonyo something?"

"Oldonyo means 'mountain,' " they explained eagerly.

"I see."

Silence again. Then it was their turn to do the questioning. The taller of the two—he spoke more than the other—cast a critical eye at the radio set.

"It must be expensive, that thing," he stated rather than asked.

"Oh yes, quite expensive."

"Two cows," he suggested.

"Ah-mm, a little less; you see, this one is quite small. Of course there are much bigger ones; some of them cost as much as eight cows."

"Wheew!!"

Yes, to them it was a fortune. Eight cows. The cow was the source and the purpose of their lives. Her death was mourned as sorrowfully as that of a human being.

Mungo was looking over the plain with what seemed to be a disturbed concentration. Engaruka, clad in brown with all her sons, was harsh; and yet fascinating. Except for that winding oasis, there was nothing inviting enough to call "home." That river basin itself was an island, not only because of its greenness which was in sharp contrast with the dry plains, but also because the people who tilled its soil were not Masai. They were people who knew the value of the soil. Every year the floods came with rich soils, and the people of the valley reaped the fruits of the river's generosity. He smiled a little when it struck him that here were black colonialists in

Masailand. Was he one of them? No, he could not see any sense in the people's existence. So enwrapped were they in themselves and their cows on these vast hot plains that they were cut off from the rest of the world. Engaruka was a place to be visited, not to live in.

But, to them, the hills, the vast plain, and the sea of brown was home; nothing unusual about them. He was a newcomer who regarded these features with a new and suspicious eye. They had known the land's scourges and sweet tempers for hundreds of years. Nothing could make them question the naturalness of so 'homely' a place; and when he asked them why they lived in such a difficult region, they were sincerely surprised.

"This has been our home for years and years," they told him, unable to get the gist of his question.

He tried an alternative, "Aren't those mountains behind us part of your land? They look greener than the plain. Here there's no rain." He might as well have asked why they were not farmers, instead of cattlemen.

Yes, they did see that the mountains were greener than the plain, (at least at that time of year), but the plain was their home, and that was that. The cow did better on these flats.

While he weighed the validity of what they had said, he was interrupted with, "Dasalamu must be very far from here," from the tall one.

"Yes it is . . . very far." It *felt* much farther than he had ever imagined before. Should he tell them how many miles? No, they would not get the idea. So he added, "Walking, you would spend about ten sunrises and sunsets to get there." They understood.

While the tall one was still agape with wonder, the short one asked, "Are there cows in Dasalamu?" which was another way of asking whether the people there had anything to live on, and to live for.

[126]

Yes, there were cows; but they were mainly kept in large houses before they were killed by a chuma for meat. Only a few people near the city kept cows. Most of them lived on rice, maize-flour, vegetables.

The Masai went apart and exchanged words between themselves for a while.

"That man is speaking from Dasalamu," said the tall one, pointing at the transistor set. Mungo was glad he was not asked how a man from Dasalamu could have his voice heard in a box so far away. They asked him to make the box sing in Swahili. He could not find a song, but he came upon one reciting a shairi.

"Is that how they sing there?" asked the short one.

"Yes." He did not want to elaborate.

At that moment they heard a droning sound overhead. It grew louder and louder. Presently, they saw a gleaming aeroplane gliding across the sky. Mungo's friends were following its progress in complete absorption, mouths agape, eyes agoggle. This was one of those rare, curious things from the other side of the world that occasionally visited their world. Like Mungo, it was an intruder.

As he observed them intently watching the plane, Mungo wondered whether the young Masai was not generally becoming interested in leaving his native regions to see a bit of the outside world. Only the previous evening he had been told (at the mission school by the river) of a young man who was being stopped from continuing his studies. He had done very well in his standard eight examinations, but his parents and the Masai elders had gone to a witch doctor to ask him to cast a spell on the young man, so that the "madness of school" would get out of his head.

Mungo could see a new eagerness in the eyes of these two young men. That they had not been to school, he could not doubt. What would they want to do, say, in Dar es Salaam? Where would they live? Who would protect them against the vices of that world?

Here on the plains, a little thorn-prick in your flesh hurt all the family. There you alone were responsible for everything you did. Yes, sooner or later, Engaruka would be touched by a new hand, and all this would come to pass. How long would it take before Engaruka was a city? A hundred years? He could not tell. Yet one day the cow would become fatter on this plain than it was then. And instead of being served by man, it would serve man. The Masai would be his own master, and then. . . .

"Motoka!" one of them nearly shouted, pointing down the hill, at an object raising a trail of dust half a mile away. Mungo recognised it as the land-rover coming for him. He smiled.

"Wananchi," he said, "I am going. That motoka has come for me. I am very pleased to have met you. I hope we shall meet again."

They smiled broadly and hoped that he would travel well. They wished he could stay a little longer among them. Would he please accept a gourd of sour milk? They could fetch it quickly. He thanked them but said he and his companion had a long way to go, and must hurry. Another time he would take the milk. He gave the tall one some coins to buy pombe, a local type of beer which he had had the evening before. He hurried down the hill, clutching his radio set under his arm, and waving to the two Masai. They watched him go.

Back in the land-rover, Mungo's mind was fertile with ideas. Here was a place to transform. That river could play a wonderful part in the plan. Engaruka could be a new place—green fields, large cattle stalls, a mean factory; electricity—new roads—hospitals—amusement parks—a sprawling trading center. With money, and people's efforts, it could be done. Let him be given the mountain for his own mansion, from where he would watch all these things happen on the plains. In ten years it would be possible—

He was rudely awakened from his dreams by the sudden halt of the vehicle. He was surprised to see that they were already halfway up the escarpment. Below them spread the deep, flat-bottomed bowl that was Engaruka. The hill that he had left half an hour ago was just a visible pimple on the flats. He wondered whether his two Masai friends were still there.

The Stone

by I. CHOONARA

There is a stone in the garden just in front of the gate.
A large stone, a boulder in fact. A large boulder. I
can't go past it. I cannot go to work. Whoever put it
there must take it away. I am not going to jump over
it or go alongside it. It is in the path and I am not going
until it is removed. There must be a way to remove it
but I am not going to do it. I did not put it there, so
why should I take it away? In any case, it is too big
and heavy for me. I have delicate hands. I cannot do
such work. My hands are unsuitable for manual work.
No, I will take my briefcase and go inside. That is all.
I am not going to do anything until that stone is removed.

"Darling, have you forgotten something," That is the
first thing she will say. Have I forgotten something.

Why should I forget something? Anything? What is there to forget? I know what I take every morning to work. I pack my briefcase. I check everything. Why should I forget? But it is the same old response: "Darling, have you forgotten something?" No, I have not forgotten anything. I am not going to work. I cannot go to work. I am feeling fine. There is a large stone in front of the gate. Right on the path. It is there, I tell you. It is there. I am not going until it is removed. I did not put it there. Why should I do it? It is not my job. Besides it is too heavy. It is not my business. I am not going to strain my back. It is a manual job. I use my brains. No, I am not going to shift it. I am not jumping over it. Not me, thank you. That would be wrong. That would be the wrong attitude. I can jump over it. I know that. I was quite good at jumping at school. I can jump over it but that isn't the point. I don't want to jump. No, I am staying right here until that stone goes.

You can't see the stone? You can't see it? Of course you can't see it. It is not there if you believe it is not there. You can't see it because you don't want to see it. It is there, I tell you. It is there. A big boulder. Yellow. Dirty yellow. Flaky in patches, but smooth. Big. Dirty yellow. You can't see a thing? Well, there is something wrong with you then if you can't see it. It is there all the time. How do I know how the milkman got past it. He probably jumped over it. Jumped over it. Dangerous with those bottles in his hands. But that is his look-out. He gets paid to deliver milk. That is his job. If he wants to jump over a boulder, that is his business. He is probably insured. By the firm. They usually do. They can afford to pay the premiums. He would get a few thousand if he broke his neck. I am not taking any risks. Besides it is undignified. Jumping over boulders in one's own front garden. And I might break my neck. And

[131]

then? What would happen to you and the kids? What would they do? Oh, they must have jumped over it also. They have gone to school so they must have jumped over it. But they are kids. They love doing things like that. They are children. It doesn't matter to them. No, I am not going to work. I do not care what they say at the office. I am not going to work. That is all. They will ring up. I will tell them. I'll tell them the truth. I'll tell them there is a big boulder in my path. Why should I tell them I have a headache? I don't have a headache. I do not stay at home because of a headache. It is dishonest. What a thing to say: I have a headache. No, I will tell them the truth. There is a boulder out there and I am not going out until it is removed. They will understand. Why should they not believe me? They are all sane people. They will understand. I'll tell them the truth. I am not telling them a lie. Why should they not believe me? No, it is not a silly reason. It is the truth. Truth is not silly. Truth is truth. Truth is beautiful. So why should it be silly. I will speak to them on the phone. Don't you worry. I'll handle this. It is my problem. You'll just muddle everything up. No, I am not going to tell them anything else. If it is not removed by tomorrow I will stay at home tomorrow also. That is the logical thing to do. What is true and reasonable today does not become untrue and unreasonable overnight.

No, children, you won't see a thing if you make up your mind not to see it. That is called selective perception. We only see what we want to see. Everything else disappears. It is the same with noise and music. We hear only what we want to hear. Everything is selective. I tell you that stone is there. You keep contradicting me. No, I do not want proof. It is there. I know it. It has been there now over a week. And all week I have had to stay at home. I know that. Do you think I like staying at home. They keep on ringing up from work, and I keep on telling them the truth. If they do not want to believe me it is their business. I cannot help them. If they want to dismiss me, they can do so. I am not worried. I am staying right here. I am not going out. That is all. Your mother says I must go to see a doctor, does she. Why should I go to see a doctor? I am not sick. There is nothing wrong with me. Why should I go and see a doctor? If I can go out to see a doctor, I can go out to work. So how can I go out to see a doctor, assuming I wanted to see a doctor? In any case, there is nothing wrong with me. Perhaps there is something wrong with you. All of you. You and your mother also. Why don't you go to see the doctor? Tell him that there is something wrong with you, that you cannot see a large boulder in the front garden. You can have your eyes tested. There is nothing wrong with mine. I can see perfectly. Yes, I can see the three fingers. All right, two fingers and a thumb. It is still only three. Very clever. There is nothing wrong with my eyesight. It is perfect. No, I am not having delusions. You both are just like your mother. I tell you that there is a boulder on the path. No, I am not coming out with you two. I am staying right here. I am not going out. I am not moving until that stone is removed. I have made my point clear. See who is on the phone. Is it for me? I'm coming.

Yes, I am fine. No, it is not silly. What my wife told you? Look, come over if you like. You will have to jump over the boulder. It is just inside the gate. Big yellow boulder. You can't miss it. Come over and we'll talk about it. Come early. All right, then you can have coffee with us. Yes, yes, Mary will be pleased to see you. It will be all right; I'm not busy. Yes, I'll see you. Remember the boulder just inside the gate. Bye then.

Yes, Bill is coming, for coffee. Why should I not tell him about the boulder? He is my friend. You are all conspiring against me. You have probably told your mother and father about it. You think I care. I tell you I don't care. I don't care for anybody. You're all against me. I know. It's some kind of trick. How do I know why you should do it? I don't know everything that you do. I don't live in your head. What did you tell them? Go on, tell me. Or are you too scared to tell me the truth? See what I mean. A simple thing like a boulder in the path and you go on distorting the truth to suit your own purpose. Well I am not being fooled by you. All of you. You'll see. Let Bill come. He is my friend. He'll back me up. You'll see. He'll be here soon. You'll see. I think there is a car stopping. I think it is his car. It is his car. The blue one. No, don't worry. I will go to the door myself. I'll let him in.

Hello Bill, glad you came. You jumped over the boulder. You are young. But I am not doing anything like that. Come in. Come in and sit down. You did jump over the boulder. Well, did you or didn't you? There is no boulder! What are you talking about? No boulder in the path! No boulder! You are on their side. I can see that. I keep telling them there is a boulder out there on the path. What is wrong with all of you. Are you all blind? I am telling you there is a large boulder out there. And I am not shifting it. That is final. No, I am not going to the office. I don't care. Why should I see a doctor. There is nothing wrong with me. I am perfectly normal. If they think that way then it is their business. I am not responsible for them. It is all a kind of conspiracy to get me out. All right, let them fire me. Who cares. I have some savings. It will see us through till this business gets cleared up. Look, Bill, you are my friend, my very good friend, and I value your advice and your opinion but so should you value mine. Friendship is both ways, is it not? Don't you see that it is you who are wrong, not me? You want to help me. I understand. That is what Mary keeps telling me. Even my children want to help me. But it is all conceit, arrogance. There is nothing wrong with me, don't you understand that? There is a large stone out there, and I am not going out until it is removed. What is more simple and straightforward than that? Yet all of you keep going on and on about seeing a doctor. I do not want to see a doctor. I do not need a holiday. I am not overworked or tired or anything else.

I am not sick, do you understand that? I am as normal as you all. I am not sick. Do you understand that? There is nothing wrong with me. You do not see a boulder. I see a boulder. Why should it be that I am wrong and you right? I see that boulder. Clear as these fingers before me. And if that boulder does not shift then I'll stay here. Tell me what is simpler than that. Tell me. Tell me. Don't just stand and stare like that. Speak. Say something. Why are you all staring like that? Don't you understand? It is such a simple thing. Such a simple thing. What can be simpler than that? You will come again, Bill, promise. It is such a simple matter. Such a simple matter. What is wrong with everybody?

Yes, you are the only friend I have, Bill. All these twenty years you have remained faithful. You come to see me, see us, regularly. Even the children don't come so often. And when they bring the little ones, they seem frightened. They talk in whispers. And then they go away. Only you come regularly. And Mary has always remained with me. She works hard. All the time. She brought the children up. They send something every month. And Mary works and that helps. I wait here with my briefcase but the stone is still there. My eyes are not so good now but I can see the stone there. All the

[135]

time. Do you think they will take it away? Are you sure? You think so, Bill. It is good to have a friend. They will take it away one day. I know they will. You think so too. I am so glad you think that way. I am so glad. I am so glad, Bill. So glad.

The River

by ELINOR SCHIFFRIN

*Ikpoba River was formed long ago by a woman
named Ogiesukhe, wife of Oba Eware of Benin.
She was not well-liked at the palace and one day,
after quarrelling with the Oba, she decided not
to be his wife any longer. So she left the palace
and the city and set off into the bush.*

*As she walked she began thinking about all
her troubles. Her greatest sorrow was that she
had no child. She sent a message to her sister,
saying that she had suffered too much and
wanted to die. She said that she was going to a
place near Ododonuwa Valley.*

*Crying bitterly, she went to this valley. On
her way she talked to God, telling Him her
troubles. Her sister came to the valley to look*

*for her, but never saw her again. Instead she
saw a small river, flowing full and gently from
the ground. Ogiesukhe had transformed herself.
This river still flows and in Benin it is called
Ikpoba!*

On Friday morning Itohan sat on a wooden packing
crate and pared oranges, cutting away the tough outer
skin, leaving only the soft yellow under-skin. She slit
the tops, leaving them in place. Penny-penny oranges
now, two-for-a-penny in season. She sat under the roof
on her stall, which was a straw mat thrown loosely over
the top of a rectangle made of four wooden sticks nailed
together. The rectangle was in turn supported by four
sticks nailed at the corners and going down to the
ground. Projecting from the front of the stall was the
table where she stacked her goods. Here, for two hours
already, her goods had been unloaded from the white
enamel basin in which she carried them from home
every day but Sunday.

Loaves of bread took more than half the space on the
table. Some of it was wrapped in printed waxed paper:
"Buy Nwaka's Delicious Sliced Super Bread—For Strength
and Vitality—Wrapped for Hygiene." The loaves were
stacked parallel, as close to each other as possible, the
second row stacked on top of the first and at right angles
to it. Most days she also had unsliced bread, brown and
sloping at the ends, tied in clear plastic bags with small
strips of printed yellow paper, the ink easily seen through
the bags: "Vero Bakery." On the paper there was also
a picture of a white angel in flowing robes, framed in
a wreath of leaves.

Itohan looked up from the orange she was paring as

she caught sight of a young boy beside her table. He was dressed for school, light brown shorts and a white shirt. Neither had been smooth and shining since the stiff cloth, run from the loom somewhere in England and brought to Nigeria in huge rolls, had been cut and finally sold from the school office in pre-ordered small boys' sizes. It was enough to wash them in the enamel basins, blue-frothed with "Omo" and water from the street tap, or even in the Ikpoba River, its own gentle heavings washing round the bathers and washers in all weathers down at the bottom of Ikpoba Slope, and then let dry, still shadowed with Benin's or Ikpoba's red dust, moulding gently in the sun to the grass's or the bushes' shape, yet holding finally the boy's own.

He stopped and asked for an orange, then put his penny in her hand. The orange was soft under his fingers. He tore off the top, squeezed the sides and sucked the juice from it, sweet and warm already in the morning sun.

"Iyare," she asked, "what of your friend? He buys two oranges from me. He is late again?" She screwed on the lid of the money tin.

"Omokaro is being punished," he answered. They were both silent. "He lost his mother's money," he added.

"Oh, sorry!" Itohan pursed her lips and made a sucking noise. "Where did he go with it?" she asked.

"He was to buy eggs. Never found the money when he got to Mrs. Odia's house." Iyare felt the sun hot on his head and shifted his school bag to the other hand. It was made of light many-colored squares of plastic and bulged with worn textbooks and exercise books.

"Sorry." Itohan shook her head and frowned deep wrinkles.

"He will be coming again," said Iyare. "I'm going now."

He joined the traffic on Ikpoba Slope. Small Morris

taxis speeded and weaved down the street, passing lorries, heavily laden on the road to Agbor, passing bicycles, pushcarts, and the pedestrians, who were mostly school children and women with headloads for market.

Itohan wrapped her lapsing headtie more tightly and shifted on the packing crate. She was a large woman and, as her son had written in an English essay fifteen years ago, "of fair complexion," which in Benin is a soft, rich brown, lighter than mahogany, darker than Nescafé sweetened with tinned milk.

"I am fair-complected as well," he had written, "but my father is very dark. My brother was dark too. And my mother walks with great dignity. . . ."

She looked over her goods now. Cigarettes were slow this week; mouths were too dry and the sun too strong. But oranges sold well during February and March. She counted her tins: ten tomato paste, twelve "Queen of the Coast" sardines, seven "Beefex" corn beef, five "Peak" milk. There were a bowl of kola, neatly piled stacks of Bisco biscuits, cylindrical tins of Flight, Gold Leaf, and Bicycle. A 100-X Shell Oil tin sprouted pale wooden chewing sticks.

It was mid-morning when a young girl came toward Itohan's stall, tired and top-heavy with a wooden, glass-fronted box on her head. "Buy buns!" she chanted in a minor key, shrill and plaintive, "Buy buns! Sweet buns!" Esohe went to school only occasionally and dressed more colorfully than the school girls in uniform maroon or blue or green. Today she wore a printed wrapper over a dress that was long reft of buttons, its wilting fabric freeing itself from the seams at her waist and under her stretched arms that reached up high to hold the box on a pad of wound cloth on her head.

She stopped and sang again at a likely customer, "Sweet buns!" They were piled, soft and crusty, to near the top of the box. The customer stopped her with a look at the box, his hand reaching into the pocket of his trousers. While Esohe heaved the box to the ground, he sorted out a brass coin and asked for a big one. She opened the lid, took a torn piece of a pool-office sheet from a stack inside the box, and wrapped it around a golden, mango-shaped bun that soon greyed the paper's surface with oil. She put his coin in the tin in her box and slowly hoisted the box back on her head.

Esohe was Itohan's granddaughter and tradition ruled that she kneel on approaching her. However, Esohe's box was heavy, Itohan's tolerance broad, and their association so constant that she kneeled to her grandmother only when a special occasion demanded it. Itohan smiled broadly now from her place under the straw mat. Her legs relaxed outward under the spread of her wrapper and her shoulders rounded forward in the bright green glow of her *buba*. Esohe walked towards her, balancing the box unconsciously. She bent her knee in a slight curtsy and greeted her warmly.

"Good morning, Grandmother!"

"Eh, good morning, Child. Did you sleep well?" she asked, as usual.

"Yes, I've slept well," Esohe answered.

"How are your feet today?" she asked, her smile fading into a concerned frown at the girl's feet. Esohe held the box with one hand and bent her left leg back from the knee to examine the underside of her toes, which had dry open crevices where they joined the ball of her foot. Then she looked at the other foot.

"Not very bad," she said. "They are very dirty. But I don't think of them. They don't hurt."

"Sit down and rest with me." Itohan offered her a smaller wooden crate beside her own. Esohe took her box down again and sat on the crate.

"What of your aunt? Osaretin is well?" Itohan asked.

"Yes, she's fine. She is plaiting one woman's hair today and the woman screams every time my aunt pulls her hair."

"So the woman will not be so happy?"

"No," Esohe answered.

"And your cousin, Omosefe, she is all right?"

Esohe paused. "Oh, yes, she is all right. But she has been bad. Last night she took all my clothes from the box. She put them in dirty water and then spread them out in the dust. I had to wash them all again." Esohe sighed.

"What a busy child! Your aunt did not beat her?"

"No, but I did myself," Esohe answered, "until Osaretin came and stopped me."

A young man came up to the stall for cigarettes and Itohan served him with her deliberate, unvarying ritual, enclosing his money in her tin, handing him his purchase. Esohe ground her heel into the dust and stared at the ground for a few seconds. Then she opened her box and took out the money tin. She spread her knees apart and poured the coins into the bowl of her skirt. There were mostly fat brown pennies with holes in the middle. She stacked them in piles of six on her legs, pressing the sides of the coins between her fingers so that they lay exactly on top of each other. She concentrated on keeping her legs still. Bending forward she could see the orange cloth of her wrapper down the holes in the centre of each pile. She sorted out the dull yellow *itoros* and divided them evenly between the pennies, placing them over the holes of each pile. There were not enough sixpence pieces to go around, so she put them back in the tin and gazed at her piles.

Business stepped up. Itohan had sold three loaves of bread, some cigarettes and a package of biscuits before she glanced at her granddaughter and stopped her reverie.

[142]

"Put them away! Little fool! You think they are stones to play with?"

Esohe started and smiled foolishly, then diverted her eyes and began to replace the coins in the tin.

A well-dressed woman glided into view and stopped to greet Itohan, relaxing the grandmother's stern face into a smile.

"Ko. . . ."

"Eh, Koyo."

"You are well?" the woman asked.

"Yes, well. And yourself?"

"Yes, well."

"You will be going to market now?" asked Itohan.

"No, I'm not for the market now," replied her friend.

They spoke warmly for several minutes while Esohe prepared to go. She returned all but the last pile of coins, which she wrapped into a careful knot in a corner of the cloth she used for a head pad. Itohan saw that she was ready to go and helped her lift the box and rest it securely on her head. Then she smiled at her through vaguely clouded eyes.

"Go well, Esohe. Sell the buns early before they stale. And take care of your aunt's money."

Esohe faced the two women. She bent her knee almost imperceptibly to them and then turned and walked slowly into the street, as smoothly and inscrutably as a young deer into the bush. Itohan's troubled eyes followed her up the road. A memory knocked dully in her mind. Yesterday Esohe had forgotten to bring home the bread her mother had ordered. One day she had found her staring at nothing, her mind gone. As if juju. . . . As if someone's juju made her forget herself.

Her friend Erhu had been speaking. Itohan began to listen again. "Her son is still sick?" she asked.

"Yes, poor woman. One trouble or another falls on

[143]

her. First she loses a week's earnings to a thief. Now the baby has a fever and coughs and frets all night. For three nights now she says she has not slept." Erhu pursed her lips and made soft clucking sounds of regret.

"Has she brought a doctor to see him?" Itohan asked, concern showing in her face.

"Yes, but none of his medicines have worked. He has come twice already."

"Let us pray he will be well tomorrow." Itohan paused. "My own son had the fever. It is no small sickness."

Erhu had forgotten Itohan's own loss. The first one—was it thirty years? she wondered, and the other just a few years ago with a high fever. She caught herself now. Too often lately she had spoken without thinking.

"God rest his soul," she offered, more in embarrassment than regret.

A lorry came down the slope, passing close to the stall and spraying fine dust over Erhu's matching blue wrapper and *buba*. She coughed and brushed her clothes with brisk, irritated slaps. She sputtered in annoyance, rattling her gold earrings.

"Sorry, sorry," said Itohan, shaking her head sympathetically.

"Too many lorries on this road," Erhu muttered. "I'll be happy for the rains to come and settle this dust."

"Yes, but the road is good for business. And you know," Itohan said philosophically, "the rain will come and you'll be complaining about the mud and the mold on your clothes." Erhu was still patting her wrapper. "Eh, Erhu, stop fretting. Your clothes are still fine."

"Of course, there is always something." Erhu picked up her plastic shopping basket, getting ready to leave. "I'm going to see if the dressmaker has finished my new blouse," she said, pulling her wrapper more tightly around her middle. "Goodbye until tomorrow."

"Greet your sister for me. Take care." Itohan had time to wave and watch her friend sweep majestically down the road as far as the Esso station before another customer came.

By the time she had finished serving him, her mind had wandered back to her granddaughter. She had been very strange lately. Esohe had never been very loud or playful. Other small children sang songs together, danced naked in the sun, taunted each other and went out in the night to catch crickets when the moon was bright. But Esohe was often alone, watching her shadow, singing quietly to herself. Sent to collect firewood, she would come back hours late without it. She was the only child of Itohan's son. When he died, Esohe's mother sent her to live with Osaretin in Benin. Esohe had been even more alone and quiet since she came to Benin, where she lived with Osaretin and Osaretin's husband and child, helped the family by selling buns and watching her cousin, Omosefe. But she puzzled everyone, became angry suddenly, sad without anyone knowing why. Itohan understood her better than anyone else, but even her grandmother wondered about her.

Itohan's memory lingered over her granddaughter before falling, as it often did, to her only children, two dead sons. One, Esohe's father, had grown and married at least, and had given her one grandchild before he died. The other, whom she mourned more bitterly, had drowned in the river; one afternoon, when he had just stopped to swim on his way home. They said he was destined for Ikpoba, and no one could unsay what the river said. Itohan resented Ikpoba: vengeful woman, she thought, jealous and cruel. But she loved the river too. How could she not love it: always flowing, washing, murmuring, softly rolling in the sun, running in the rain. But reverence is fear for such a river; with drums beating in the water. You hear them in the morning. No men made that song; people don't dance that way.

At twenty she was dancing herself. A hundred friends followed with her husband to his home. A hundred friends heard his grandmother's prayers for their marriage and many children. At forty with one granddaughter, she was dancing seldom. This noon, under the sunstruck straw mat she danced not at all, though lorries, taxis, bicycles, all danced through the swimming vision of her eyes.

By mid-afternoon Itohan was dozing fitfully, bent over her table. She had shifted the loaves of bread to make room for her arms, on which she rested her head. Traffic up the hill had slowed. The men working on the road had stopped for their dinner and siesta. The sun beat everywhere. No breeze lifted the edges of her straw hat. which hung wasted and scorched over the stall, providing shade but no comfort underneath. The smell of sliced pineapples and pared oranges hung heavy in the air, rotting and rising in the heat.

Itohan raised her head from her arms, feeling the dull discomfort of the afternoon. She felt old. Lately she had begun to dread the long walk home at night, when she and her friends loaded their heads with the enamel basins and unsold goods and filed slowly through the streets, talking softly now and then, avoiding bicycles, and turning their heads when the heavy lorries came by.

Tomorrow she would go to market, buy peppers and yam, rice, garri, other things which she did not grow at home, some little present for her granddaughter, maybe some cloth. She looked forward to seeing her friends, women of her own age whom she had known all her life. They would talk of their relatives and of business, of new babies, motor accidents, thefts, all the news of the week. She was tired and dozed again, her mind troubled in half-dreams with thoughts of Esohe.

A block and a half away Esohe watched a girl her own age haggle with a vendor for a piece of fish. The girl sold rice, each portion wrapped in a large *ebieba* leaf (soup added free) for a penny. She wanted to trade two for a piece of fish. The offer was rejected. A piece of fish cost one *itoro* and the fish seller wanted one penny in rice and two in cash, which he finally got.

Esohe ate nothing, although her aunt had been firm and annoyed that morning, when she packed Esohe's box:

"Now, I'm giving you twenty large buns and thirty-four small," she had said. "You bring me seven shillings, ten pence or the leftover buns. And don't make any stories for me about losing the money or giving away too much change."

Omosefe had been fretting on the floor.

"And be sure you eat something today, Esohe. I don't want you coming home like a hungry dog. Spend six pence and put some food in your stomach." She had shut the lid of the box and helped Esohe settle it on her head.

Omosefe had begun to cry and her mother stopped to feed her some garri. At this reprieve Esohe had turned quietly and left the house, eluding further benefit of her aunt's lecture.

Now Esohe was hardly even tempted to unroll the coins from the cloth on her head, though she had no purpose in saving them, at least as far as she knew. She had several shillings worth of other coins, wrapped in a fancy scrap of cloth and buried in the compound. She would add these to them.

By four o'clock Esohe was tired of carrying, of calling for customers, of walking. She sat down on the cement stoop in front of the Supreme Fotos shop. If my feet were in the river now, she thought, and my legs in the water too . . . my dress stuck wet to me, so cool now. When I talked about going, Grandmother said, "Absolutely no!" But I went anyway. And Osaretin told me: "You come sit in the tub if you want a bath. Now go fetch water from the tap and don't forget to turn it off!" But last week, every week now, I go down the slope to the river on Saturday. Saturday is a good day. Just cool water on a hot day.

Now she was bored and restless. Maybe, she thought, maybe I'll go today. But she felt a soft pang in her stomach and knew it would soon be time to walk towards home. She lifted the box to her head and began walking towards Forestry Road.

She got to her uncle's compound before dark, perhaps a dozen unsold buns yet in her box, oily and stale. Her wrapper hung loosely and she dragged her feet in the dust in front of the house. Omosefe came out to greet her, chattering in her own version of Bini and pulling at Esohe's dress, trying to bring the box down.

"Wanta eat bun! Wanta eat bun!"

She was a well-fed child and probably would eat no more than a bite if she got a bun. However, Esohe liked giving her food, making her repeat special words and gestures to get it.

"Osaretin!" she called out, "Can I give Omosefe a bun?"

"What? You have buns left again today?" her aunt called from the door.

"Only a few. Can Omosefe have one?"

"Yes," she answered. She was tired. "Did you have any yourself? Did you have anything today, like I told you?"

Esohe's face was turned. She was busy counting the remaining buns. "Yes," she lied.

"What did you eat?"

[148]

"I had a piece of fish and some rice and soup." Esohe took out a bun for her cousin. She felt her aunt's eyes on her and decided to forgo the usual "say please" ritual.

"Well, then you won't be too hungry now," Osaretin said. "And that's good, because there's only a little garri. Will that be enough for you?"

Esohe fought with herself. "Yes," she said, trying to sound indifferent, "it will be enough. I'm not hungry."

She took the buns and followed her aunt into the house. She smelled cooked meat as soon as she came into the dark room and then remembered that the cooking fire had been burning in the yard.

"What's that meat?" she asked. "Is my uncle having guests?"

Osaretin was lighting the kerosene lamp and waited until the small flame rose to a glow on her face.

"No, that's no food for guests." She paused, her eyes narrowed intently on the flame, and turned the small rod to adjust it.

"It's for Olokun."

Now it was light enough for Esohe to see a large leg of antelope on a tray, steaming and well-browned in the lampglow.

Esohe, like all children she knew, were taught early not to touch food which they were not given. But food for the juju was especially forbidden, so much that it seemed to them not even to be food. Its taste would be for a god's mouth, its warm filling weight for a god's stomach, so even its smell was for this god's nose, and not for their own. So the strong steaming smell would seldom waken a child's appetite when it came from meat cooked for juju.

But Esohe smelled the meat tonight and she was hungry. She smelled cooked antelope and it smelled good. This came to her mind with the knowledge that it was for juju and set up a clamouring in her head that made her leave the room in a raging sense of impotence and disbelief. She stormed to the back of the house.

"Omosefe!" she cried from the doorway, "Come here now! And bring that bucket behind you!"

She watched her two-year-old cousin raise her head slowly, distracted from the piles of stones she was playing with. Omosefe gazed wide-eyed and wondering at Esohe and made no movement to get up.

"You little goat! What are you staring at?" Esohe screamed. "Bring me that bucket now!"

Omosefe had her own moods. She pressed her lips together and looked down at the stones in the dust between her legs. Esohe's anger overran her now, brimmed and flowed in a hot surge of injured pride and hate for the little goat who sat unmoved by her passion.

Omosefe saw her coming in the light of the cooking fire and tensed her body in a scream. Esohe was more insensed by this cry and slapped Omosefe on its piercing crescendo. Then the night was pitched into a volley of screams that burst from each other, swelling to the furthest edge of firelight and fainting in the dark beyond. Osaretin was outside as soon as she heard the first note of Omosefe's wail. She saw Esohe slap her and screamed at her to stop. She ran to the children, seized the baby and shrieked at Esohe, who shrieked back. Then she beat Esohe, who had never stopped screaming since she had slapped Omosefe.

Osaretin, ruffled and angry, and still shouting high-pitched abuse at Esohe, carried Omosefe into the house to comfort and feed her. Esohe, her pride seared, but not badly hurt from the beating, gathered herself into a self-consoling crouch under a small tree. She sat with her knees up to her face, her face buried in the cloth of her wrapper and her arms clutched around her legs, holding them close to her chest.

Osaretin, quietly feeding Omosefe, was less troubled by her baby's easily quieted sorrows than by Esohe's mysterious passion. She tried to remember if she had seen any signs of it before, if Esohe had seemed unwell or had acted strangely. Why would she beat Omosefe? "Bring me the bucket behind you," she had said. And when I was lighting the lamp I told her, "It's for juju." She is not normal tonight. Is she hungry? Did she have any food today?

Esohe felt the blood in her head subside; her sobs dwindled to self-conscious sniffles. Still clutching her legs to her chest, she rocked her body back and forth. She raised her head and looked at the lights, which through her tears were bright needle points threaded like spiderwebs. Two feelings were left in her now: hunger and desire for revenge. She got up and wiped her nose with her wrapper. From the back room of the house she heard her aunt's voice as she talked softly to Omosefe. Listening carefully for any change in the sound of her voice, Esohe moved quietly around the house, giving it wide berth. Standing in front of the house she could see the small lamp her aunt had lit, on the floor of the front room. It glowed on the brown walls and floor of the room, lit up a few pieces of wooden furniture and the blue cloth that hung in the doorway to the next room. Beyond its brightest glow she saw the shining rim of the tray that held the cooked antelope meat. She saw that it was all ready but knew that it would not be offered until early in the morning.

Esohe, moving close to the house, watched the space under the cloth that hung in the inside doorway, and still heard every sound in the house. For an instant she paused on the stone step before the entrance to the house, then glanced quickly behind her. Nothing had changed. She darted into the room, making almost no sound on the floor, and lifted the meat from the tray. It was heavy. She clutched it carefully in both arms and in five or six seconds was out of the house again. There was a small bush a few yards from the house and she ran towards it now, blindly in the dark.

Itohan's compound was a long way from Oba's Market. She got up earlier than usual next morning to make the walk. She dressed carefully, tying a huge brown wrapper over a *buba* of the same color, its soft and heavy bulk adding to her own. She tied her headtie in generous, overlapping folds so that it rose higher than usual on her head. She left instructions with the small boy who watched her house, and took her enamel basin for carrying home the things she would buy.

It was still early when she arrived at the market and not all the stalls were open yet. She decided to visit her friend, Aiyoweren, at her stall, where she would be able to sit and rest for a while. When she came to the stall to greet her, Itohan met Erhu and another woman already visiting with Aiyoweren. They were seated and talking excitedly with mobile faces, interrupting each other often.

The three woman saw Itohan and stopped talking at once. A troubled silence enveloped them, then Erhu broke it:

"Ah, Itohan! Sorry, sorry!" she cried.

"Come sit here." The other woman gestured to the space beside her on a wooden chest.

Itohan drew her eyes together and smiled at them doubtfully. "Eh, good morning! Why sorry? No trouble, eh?" She put her basin on the ground and drew her wrapper around her before sitting on the chest.

Aiyoweren frowned deeply, as if to withdraw from the scene they had begun and could no way stop. Itohan faced the three women directly now, her elbows on her knees. Her face was thrust forward and open in question, a dim fear looming from the back of her eyes.

"What trouble? You were saying to me . . ."

"You don't know?" Erhu cried in disbelief.

"About Esohe?" said Aiyoweren.

"No! What about Esohe?" Itohan cried, the shadow in the back of her eyes growing darker. "Last night? What . . . ?"

"She thieved the meat for juju," Aiyoweren said, measuring each word with soft restraint.

Now Itohan was incredulous. Her jaw dropped and she shook her head. "No! Not a thief! Esohe is not a thief!"

"Her aunt told me this morning," said the third woman. "We heard Esohe crying all the way down the street and she never stopped when we were at the house."

"What did Osaretin do to her?" Itohan could hardly form the words in her mouth.

"You know what they used to do?" said Erhu.

Itohan remembered and closed her eyes.

"No! Osaretin didn't do that!"

Erhu continued, "If a child stole from juju, the mother would pound a nail into his head. They would throw him into the road and wait for him to die."

Itohan fell forward.

"Hush, Erhu!" Aiyoweren cried, grasping Itohan by the shoulders. "No! It is not true. Osaretin did no such thing! Esohe cried because her aunt rubbed pepper in her eyes."

Itohan tried to sit up straight. "Rubbed pepper in her eyes? Oh God! That child . . ." Itohan's eyes were vacant now. The faces of the three women swam before her. "And she cried and cried . . . ?" Itohan's voice hung on the question and faded off.

"Already this morning she has been sent away to live with Osaretin's brother in Ologbo," the third woman said.

The three women were silent. One of them finally got up and found a taxi to take Itohan home.

Late in the afternoon Iyare saw Itohan on Ikpoba Slope. She was walking downhill, very slowly and stopping every few steps. He was puzzled. His father had sent him to the sawmill on an errand, so he decided not to run down the hill and greet her. But the sight of her stayed in his mind and later he went down to ask of her. It was late by now and he saw none of the usual crowd of people who used the river for washing and bathing. Itohan had been there, one man said, but Iyare never saw her again.

Ogiesukhe had become the river and so it was now. Itohan joined her, they said, swelled the river, her own soul carried in the current with hers, in gentle and unending flow from Utekon to Obazagbon.

DRAMA

and

FILMS

Ballad of the Cells
A PHYSIOLOGY IN TWENTY-SEVEN
PULSES AND A CHORAL ELEGY

by COSMO PIETERSE

PULSE 1

NARRATOR

Alone;
His ghost haunts me,
Nor will it leave you alone
Till his restless corpse
Tall spirit
Is grown
Beyond dark taunts in
Fenced cities, bitter drops
To its own bright station
Within our possible time
That we will inherit
The ageless all we
Whose reasoned elation
Is rhymed, timeless, sublime:
And his spirit a sole

Elegiac tree
Whose far roots fuse
To its tall stem
Past and present and whole
And its rhythmical leaves
On branches of loves
That labor for use
And tomorrow lives
Dividual mass
Clusters and cells
Spring budding and birth
Ripe time, flower's death
And the high hymn
And the hard seed
Simple pure rhyme
Plural coiled sound
Birds sing on
Their will winging
Sing on the wing and
Over all lands
And over the epic nest
In the poised
Pinnacled noiselessly
Perfective cypress
That may move grains of soil
In our earth, and compass
Even round space
And space so high
In the wind and its wide
World wandering voice
Over green graves
Which hold the rest
Of the nameless brave
Whose unknown death
Seed stifled in sand
Find symbol and name

In Looksmart's last breath
His deathless zest
Living timeless gust:
Individual time
Rings,
And rings
That time won't toll,
But will chime
Names and his mates
His mate
And his name
And sings
His all
Love, faith, his mate
And hope
Though alone . . . . . .
Without sleep,
And alone
He waits

PULSE 2

LOOKSMART

No married love beside my sleep
Only bland mirrors multiply
Glib answers hollow echoes keep
Wide silences reply and die.

LOOKSMART

"I am no criminal. I'm a man."

INTERROGATOR

YOU ARE A MAN. QUITE. ALL IS WELL.

LOOKSMART

"Why kraal me as an ox alone?"

INTERROGATOR

THIS IS *YOUR* CELL; NO KRAAL, NOR HELL.

LOOKSMART

No feet beside my pacing, halted march
Only dim murmurs that divide
My mind from me and overarch
The cell where Looksmart tried and died.

LOOKSMART

"The world's beside: We're not alone."

INTERROGATOR

ALONE? NO, NOT ALONE. ALONE.

LOOKSMART

"They hear my cell, our country groan."

INTERROGATOR

AND STAND ASIDE; LEAVE YOU ALONE.

LOOKSMART

No man is islanded if hope
Oceans his lone peninsula.
Some armied hinterland trains slop-
Ing hills, trains . . . .

INTERROGATOR

WHAT TRAINS! WHERE?

PULSE 3

LOOKSMART

Rails gleam the addered distances
That summer's speed sloughs off in time:

[160]

The winter's sleep: resistance is
The ultimates this life must rhyme:
A spring tensed now against your crime.

PULSE 4

LOOKSMART

Against two children cradled in my arms,
And both my arms; for manhood speaks:
(Both ambushed arms, and all at rest . . . .)
Present arms, fall out, stand at ease?
All arms embodied every day;
Days grow to all the lengths of weeks
Throughout the weakening of the moon,
And every month aches yearning time.
Bulls gore red earth my daughter's blood.
The round year spills its month of days:
The madnesses of lunar length
That drain the country of its men:
Three months are ninety days that drag
Through Worcester's trained valleys of vine;
The mountains of the witch are high
But valleyed with autumnal time
And valiant for the round sky's dome.

PULSE 5

High flat Karoo:
Dry roof:
Dull mouth of fear;
Wide house of drought
Dead leaf . . . . . . :
Autumnal year;
Dumb, windy flood . . . .
Where am I here?

Why I
Why am I
Why
Here
Without my time
And sphere
Across a cross
Traced by
The snake's riveting length.
Tranced by
The river's snaking eye
That trails
The rails
And wings of flight
Trans-
Vaal
Or
Kei
The prey-filled flame
The bright
Hawkeye
The fielded mule-yoked ox
Hokaai
My child.
Why
Wife
And where
The summer
Rained:

PULSE 6

Green frogs hurrahing storms;
The purple quiet of this night
Assumes tubular hollow, hidden forms

Of lucent moonbeams, soundless flight

Where moths were celebrating light
The nuptial dance of earth and warm,
Pure, sunslaked space, freed from the tight
Cocooning coil, the larval lust.

The stormy, pulseless dongas stream
Continual the veinous clay;
Blue nightmare lungs of ocean suck, leak, swim,
Cough blood, sink; seaweed greens away.

PULSE 7

Away
Another cell
Of life
Away
Ebb briny tide
Blue moon
Of blood
My barren wife
The brackish spring's
A city
Oh! a way
Of life
Away
On swell
Of ocean's waters
Pity
Sway
Of ocean's fall
Spring's nubile
Daughters
Sand

And
Dead day

PULSE 8

Groined flesh is warm
Round circled walls
The angled wall
Is cosily and moistly soft

But cobwebs sit
And subtly spin
And stalk
Light to design and dust to sift
Branched shadows dancing patterned silk
The spider's hair, eyed, spun, is talk
Four walls
Of lonelinesses
Baulk:

PULSE 9

INTERROGATOR

YOUR ROOM'S THIS SINGLE YELLOW EYE,
INFLAMED WITH SLEEPLESS TONGUES THAT
PRY.

LOOKSMART

"My father's home will keep me sane."

INTERROGATOR

YOUR FATHER'S HOME! THE MISSION
BELLS . . . . . .

LOOKSMART

"The homing cattle lowing rain . . . . . .
Smell the fresh streams, full wells, ..."

[164]

INTERROGATOR

WHAT ELSE?
HUH? WHAT EXCEPT AN EMPTY-WOMBED,
WEEPING AND DARKLY LONGING LOVE?
FRESH STREAMS BRIM RICH. BUT YOU ARE
ROOMED HERE IN THIS CELL, WITHOUT . . . .
ALL LOVE.

PULSE 10

LOOKSMART

"My love's a city's floral flame at night;
Paint's color sung through gusts of time;
The focal breath of beaming light, a name;
My tawny lioness rhymes all her lust,
       Still haunting mine.

A flower and an animal,
A parable, a decimal,
The integrating swell, the fall
That matter drains sub-minimal."

INTERROGATOR 2

ABSOLUTE BULL:
CREATED BY LOVE'S ABSTRACT FOOL.

LOOKSMART

"My love's the candled aloe hour that blooms
Over stone tortoise shelled for peace;
Green gleaming lights, gloom on the land;
Flames soon released from hell,
       Not daunting mine."

INTERROGATOR 3

IF THE AFFLATUS JUST AIN'T DIVINE
CALL BACCHUS AND AT 10 TO 9

[165]

YOU'RE BALLY CERTAIN SURE TO SIGN:
SPIRITS ARE WILLING, AND SO FINE
DISTILLED IN MAGIC-COUGH BRANDY-WINE.

LOOKSMART

"Florence and Mona
Ray, Leonora
Essence and aura
Earth and its daemon
Leon and Lionel
And Leonardo
Lone tortured beauty
Jamilla and Helen."

INTERROGATOR 1

IS LOVE THAT FABLED TOWN WHOSE TRAGIC
    FACE
WAS woman's labor and man's WORK
EDEN AFTER THE GLISTENING SNAKE
LACCOON'S PERISTALTIC PYTHONED GUTS
HERCULES WRITHING IN HIS SHIRT
The leaping flames whose lust and gRACE
Make CLASSIC MARBLE of OUR name, the dirt
And rubble of this shame, our PAIN AND smuts.

INTERROGATOR 2

OH, NOW YOU'RE POLITICKING, BOY?
WELL, WATCH YOUR STEP.

INTERROGATOR 1

WE'LL TELL YOU HOW
THE GRADUAL MOUNTAIN-CLIMBING SAINT
    OF PEACE
WHOSE INTEGRATING MIND FORSOOK
HIS NATION, USED HIS SLOW DEGREES
TO LOOSE DARK DEATH.

[166]

AND ALSO BONDELZWART, BULHOEK.

LOOKSMART

"We knew the subtle snake that crawled
Past Kasteel's Poort's altars of stone;
We knew the fanged, forked tongue that called
Death's voluntary apple meat, and bleached the bone."

PULSE 11

INTERROGATOR 4

BUT WE . . . . TODAY WE SPEAK AS MAN TO
    MAN.
WE GIVE YOU VOTES, GOVERNMENT, LAND.

LOOKSMART

"Yes, Bah! bah! Black man
Will you get a vote?
In 'Yes Baas'—Baahntustan
Of sheep-in-sheep's coat
Chief—Caesar—Headman
Foot—man—fool
Of the brand-new ethnican-
Niballistic school!"

INTERROGATOR 2

"DAMN YOUR BLOODY CHEEK, YOU . . . ."

NARRATOR

Lightning hands
Turn the dumb cheek's unsluicing blood
To blind, gashed anger, but the sands
Of pain absorb the lonely flood.

INTERROGATOR 2

"WHO ARE THE JEWS THAT PAID YOU, KAFFIR?"

[167]

LOOKSMART

They're named—democracy and hunger.

INTERROGATOR 3

"WHICH COOLIES RAPED YOUR NAKED
MOTHER?"

LOOKSMART

Redress her congressed limbs, my love, my anger.

INTERROGATOR 3

"WHAT BASTARD HOTNOT'S GUTS CAN
FIGHT?"

LOOKSMART

Freedom has chartered many freights.

INTERROGATOR 2

"BLACKBUM KAFFIR, HAM'S SON OF NIGHT!"
Time sings, and strikes: (Midnight!) and waits . . . . .

LOOKSMART

(A single moth could give me life:
Moths come from shadowed places. Here
Blank walls are raped by blind, cold light.
Warmth has no still, cool places here.)

INTERROGATOR 4

YOU HEARD THAT . . . . . Y GAVE EVIDENCE!?
Herds of battle, birds of our will.
YOU HAVE HEARD . . . . . Z BY ANY CHANCE?!

LOOKSMART

"Yes, I have heard. Be still!"

LOOKSMART

Names sing a melody
Timeless amorphous
Ngoika and Kreli
Caved Batwa, Dingani,
Bambatta and Ghandi
Conductive to norms
Surnames and nicknames
Forms, farms, times! fames
Notions, names, nations
(Amandhla!) Isawandhla
Assagai's impi
Shield, axe and kierie
Drums of our feet
And the arms of our mind
Mandela, September,
Bunting and Cissie
Bardien and Barney,
Sisulu, Luthuli
(Uhuru!) Maburu
AND names sneer disharmony
Arlow, Barlow, Botha
Sickness on malady
Coop our coffins
Iron pounds gold
Grey, Hertzog, Rhodes,
Silence enormous
Smuts, Tulbagh, Malan
Breaking our forms
Invasions of time
In clamour cacophonous
Strijdom, Matanzima
Gold, silver, copper,
Nossel, Vinoos, Golding:
What forms for names!

AND names to rhyme forms:
"Moses Kotane said . . . ."

"CAUGHT ANY FISH TODAY?"

"C'MON, LOOKSMART, YOU'RE A CLEVER FEL-
LOW. MAKE A STATEMENT, MAN. DON'T BE
YELLOW WE'LL PROTECT YOU FROM . . . ."

LOOKSMART
The rainbow's arch
Green, violet, rose;
Time's forward march?
And my eyes close . . . . .

INTERROGATORS 1/3
COME, FELLOW, COME
DON'T PLAY THE DUMB
SENSELESSLY NUMB
GAMES YOU OPOSSUM.

INTERROGATOR 4
"OPEN YOUR EYES . . . .
YES, OPEN YOUR EYES, NGUDLE, LOOK . . . ."

LOOKSMART
My eyes are inward, still.

INTERROGATOR 4
"THIS STATEMENT MUST CONVINCE YOU
THAT WE TOOK . . ."

LOOKSMART
Life from us, land, love, will.

[170]

PULSE 13

LOOKSMART

(Light from us gone
To give us terror;
Lion and buck from tawny
And tall green forests of fire.

Moths in the mirror;
Curtains are drawn:
Reflection on fur or
The nightmare of dawn?)

INTERROGATOR 4

"DO YOU HEAR US?"

NARRATOR

He stirred,
His lips were a whimper;
His will was so limp a
Whisper concurred:
"I hear you . . . . I hear . . . . I have heard . . . ."

PULSE 14

LOOKSMART

"I have heard . . . . song
  People sing . . . .

SOLO-SINGING

  All over this land:

CROWD-SINGING

Boss is in the parlor
  AFRIKA!

Mayor Police Mission

Games Game Liquor
Parliament in session
Laws or wette

Still—Nkosi sikelele
  Xhosa, Nama, Zulu
    AFRIKA!

Hear the bells all tolling
  SPONONO—WAM
    AFRIKA!

Our mares are foaling
  Jonah—yo!
In the park that mists are
  Covering still

So—Nkosi sikelele
  Swazi and Ndebele
  Coolie, Pondo, Sutu
  Griqua, Colored, Jew, Maburu.
Oh Nkosi—all abantu
FOR ABA-NTU ARE MEN

SOLO

It won't be long
When bells shall ring
All over this land.

LOOKSMART

Yes, I have heard
That man is man
For all time
Each name, all colors and all lands . . . ."

SOLO

THEN

   [172]

Hiza Moya
Come now spirits
Joyous pleasure
O'er erst desert
Till our future
We'll fear nothing
LAW'S IN

SOLO

Our fair land

CROWD

O'ER MEN
Oh! man
O—Men
Ah—men:
All men are men.
Amen

LOOKSMART

"I am a man."

PULSE 15

INTERROGATOR 2
"THE BASTARD'S FAINTED. KICK HIS GUTS."

NARRATOR
Dull pain suffuses half-dead dust
Until redoubling life is thrust
Through each foot, on the groin's moist ruts,
Upon held hands shocked into fists
In sharp, electric cataracts, in fits
That flood the spasmed body, rake
Poor naked, tortured earth to rock

Of muscle that succumbs to pain's
Hailstones of words, showering rains,
Whipping blind questions through his face:

INTERROGATOR 2
"TRUST COOLIES? OR THE BASTARD RACE?"

INTERROGATOR 3
"BABIS WHO FLEECE YOU THROUGH THE YEAR
IN FILTHY SHOPS, OF HARD EARNED PENCE!?
AND COONS CAVORTING FROM THEIR FEAR
OF LIFE IN 2 DE NUWE JAAR'S WILD, LURID
PRANCE?"

LOOKSMART
"New Year was music, and no class
Of man exists or will; we all sang there, together, danced,
And earlier leveled living grass,

INTERROGATOR 3
(ALL FLESH IS GRASS, YOUR BIBLE SAYS!)
And later while limbs fused and glanced

INTERROGATOR 2
('A FUCKING BLOWN FUSE, WHAT DAMN
JAZZ!')

LOOKSMART
And lit the laughter of new time
Where foot and hand and mouth will rhyme
Heaven's promise, all-arching rain:
'Past lands, ploughed, husband time's new gain,'

The suburb sang and Table Bay
Swerved passionate and graceful waves
Beneath the mountains austere gray
As day broke pearly in its caves.

New Year devoted us to years
Resolved to new years' rising slopes:

LOOKSMART AND ECHO TO INTERROGATOR 1
FUNDRAISING PARTIES. THAT HOUSE . . .
WHERE. . . 'WHERE?' 'A WHITE SUBURB?'
COULD YOU LIVE THERE!"

INTERROGATOR 4
"My silence sings, my fancy gropes
My life did, friends, our plans, our hopes . . . . ."

(From this point the voices of Interrogators 1 and 4
fuse with the thoughts of Looksmart from a gradual
interruption to the point where what they say is the
burden and his thoughts are only an echo of their
statements.)

"WHAT PLANS?" DARK SUBWAY. SPRAYGUNS.
   "WHO. . .
USED YOU to shoulder TELL-TALE hills while he
WHILE HE PERHAPS KEPT SAFE *HIS* HOME?"
May tunnel safely home; while he . . . . .

"DUPLICITY DEPLOYS DISCIPLES DUMB
JEWS' JUDAS SILVER, STOCK AND PILE E-
RODE YOUR LAND, GOLD SHARES. SHARES?
THEY RISE AND RIDE. YOU STAY THEIR ARSE.
THEY RISE AND RIDE YOU! AND YOU COME
DUMB BUMPKIN UNCLE TOM JIM JOHN BOY
   COME
COME DON'T BE A FOOL." WHILE HE . . . WHY
   LEAVE
THEM SAFELY STAY AT COZY HOME
HOME STAY YOUR HOME
   WHY STAY AT HOME

[175]

SAFELY THEY HOME
FATHER SANE HOME
HERE HAVE AS HOME
WARM SMOKE IN HOME
    HO . . . SMO
    "Say No!"
    OLD WILY
        GNOME
AU TATE—WAM
HOME HEAVEN HAVEN HOME
    "SMOKE?"
        "Ta."
        Ah   JA.

INTERROGATOR 4
"AH! YES, YOUR FATHER'S HOME WILL KEEP
YOU SANE."

LOOKSMART
"My father's home? The mission bells?"

INTERROGATORS 4/1
"THE CATTLE LOW, GLISTEN HOME RAIN,
SMELL THE RICH MILK, FULL UDDERS, ..."

LOOKSMART
"And what else?"

PULSE 16

INTERROGATORS 1/3
SUMMER, AND SUN, AND LAZY, DROWSY SIN,
    AND JOYS
WHERE BEES AND BUDS MAKE DIZZY HOUSES
    FLOWERS,
THE LION'S HONEYED SWEETNESS STINGLESS
    FLOWS
OUT OOZY GOURDS OF GOLD

[176]

Yet life empowers
Slaves to sing empires low;
Worker bees to sting their drones;
Joshua's trumpet shrill to blow
Strong arms and lips to blast high thrones,
Building the days greener, to grow . . . .

Cells to besiege invading germs;
Guerilla war to choose its single terms;
Till peaceful flutes and roses glow . . .

INTERROGATOR 3

DAY AFTER DAY YOU SWEAT AWAY
GORILLA WHEREFORE IN WHO'S ZOO?
WHILE THAT PLUCKY SAM KAHN,
WILY YUSUF DADOO

INTERROGATOR 2

SIT FARAWAY OVER THE OCEAN;
PAUSE FAR TOO LONG OVER THE SEA;
SHIT RESOLUTE MOTION ON MOTION;
PISS COOLIES AND JEWS C.O.D.
PASS COOL JAW, YOU FOOL: SPIEL THEIR
    BLOODY BOLONEY
WHILE IN A GAOL CELL FAR AWAY, LONELIER
    THAN LONELY
YOU, MY BOY, POOR BLACK BOY, YOU AND YOU
    AND YOU ONLY! . . . . .
OH BRING BACK BRAVE BARNEY TO ME!

LOOKSMART

Through laboring, the sun shines glistening dew
Through mist and moist over a thousand valleys

[177]

Pregnant between ten thousand hills in
The province of birth from the sea
Mist pouring beneficence
Through groves of pineapples
Plantations of sugar
Sweet for all people
Tropical breasts fruit
The tall women
From over the sea
Now native here
Mildewed
Exiles
Or
Proud
From the
North
Natal
Gave
Them
Birth

INTERROGATOR 4

"DO YOU REMEMBER '49 WHO MURDERED
A BANTU BOY, TILL THE ZULUS FED THE
  EARTH
WITH FLAMES AND THE FAT CURDLED
MILK OF INDIAN PROFIT AND FEAR? YOUR
  GIRTH
IS THIS BRAVE COUNTRY. WHO HERDED
PROUD CATTLE AND WARRIORS HERE FROM
  THE NORTH?"

LOOKSMART

"Natal gave all birth."

INTERROGATOR 2

"GIVE HIM THE WORKS, THE CHEEKY, STUB-
BORN BASTARD!"

PULSE 17

The writhing body's spasm shocks
Barren conception of his life:
Erect, impotent generation mocks
The mind, the muscle's nervous strife.

But out of these antitheses
The spirit's contrapuntal theme
Rises in rhythmic melodies
Whose climax is the life of him,
For unorgasmic ecstasies,
Erect, indetumescent, climb.

LOOKSMART

That lovely old sun keeps breaking through
A blessed thousand days and bays
Urgent embracing capes, green inlets who
Shell-scape this province of good hope
Inside sweet waters, rain, sweet sea and dew
Must pouring stills munificent
In vineyards and orchards
Of plums and sweet
Dust blooming purple
Slave seed and herdsman
And hunters and exiles
And dead hunters
And the profuse
Mixture of this
Rich Cape of
Hope of
Various
Life's
Long
Plenteous
Horn

"AH HA! BUT WHERE IS MASILO NOW?
AND WHO IS YOUR GIANT IN OUR OLD STORY?
WHO IS THIS HEAVENLY MASILONYANE?
WHY HAS HE, (HEY, HAS HE?) BEEN GIVEN
THE WHITE COW?"

LOOKSMART

"Our Father . . ."

INTERROGATOR 4

"WE ARE SONS OF THE SAME FATHER?
IN HEAVEN YES! BUT
MASILONYANE'S IS NOT ALL AFRICA
DO NOT CROSS THE RIVER
LOOKSMART, NGUDLE, MASILO, MY SON,
THOSE WHO EAT FISH . . . . .
THEY ARE YOUR BIG BROTHER
WHO CAN EVENLY PLOUGH EVEN THE WATER.
THEY WILL EAT WITH YOU, FROM YOUR
   NATION'S DISH
AND DRINK FROM YOUR BOWL,
SITTING ROUND THE RONDAVEL,
THE REBUILT LAPA, HERE, HERE IN OUR
   ROUND HUT.
AND WE SHALL MAKE THE ROUND TABLE . . ."

LOOKSMART

Spiders moving along the wall,
Longlegged, weighing, waiting, dance;
Upon what innocent of ill
Filigree wing will fine silks pounce.

Feathers dust moistly underarm
In builded and fine angled art

To promise beds of coolth from harm
In web disturbed mind's hungry heart.

WHEN WILL YOUR HAND FASHION YOUR WILL?

They swim. I sink and drink thick slime.

WHAT WOMB CAN PRISONED LOINS "COMPEL"?

She calls. I fall.
"NOW IS THE TIME."

Time is the gust of moving things,
Rhyming red rust on minute wings
Whose flight's fine as a feather sings:
Dead living dust like crystals, hair,
The burning lust of lungs for air
Turning, and yearning . . . time will bear.
Soft warmth sifts from life's muscled wave
And recreative sleep webs flesh:
Sweet life subtly suffuses limbs through meshed
Time's womb; dust proves deepest, osmotic love.

PULSE 18

Creative oceanic sleep in his;
Great walls, floors, turrets of his dreams
Glisten widely, clamor with bliss:
Day climbs, life builds, and teams and teems.

[181]

Rich, creamy udders tugged by young
Calves hungering for running love;
Gleaming machineries hum their deep, unending song
Of laughing labor's chugging drive.

Below the chuckle of the hands,
Below care's cheerful tongue that proves,
Below the probing eyes that dance;
Above . . . . . time's syncopating, breathing mind:

As coil on coil our deeds unwind
The shrouds around the dead romance
Until its murdered Looksmart moves
Rhythmic courage to symphonies
Of flowering desert and sweet seas—
The choral ONWARD of all lands.

PULSE 19

NARRATOR

Pretoria's jacarandas wake:
Verandahlese Cape-Dutch facade
Achelessly branches purple, rak-
Ing claws through this Republican Volkaraad

To level every irrigated rood
That laws have ploughed and M.P.'s sowed
With the quiescent and the urgent seed
That always flowers purple blood.

The day interrogates the sun;
The sun beats violent flowers down
Until the violet middays run
Over Marabastad from the town.

PULSE 20

LOOKSMART

They dance confined in township, in
The tourists' eye, to drum and flutes:
The song within my living skin
Is penny-whistled, whispered, mute.

INTERROGATOR 1

WHAT IS YOUR DEATH TO THEM?

LOOKSMART

Death is compounded theirs in mine;
Gold miners long for light and time
While phthisis picks them, pocking skew the long lung's
    finite, infinitely fine rhythm.

PULSE 21

NARRATOR

The evening questions all his blood;
Blood runs to faltering, nervous thrill;
Young body's thrill is understood
To undermine the bearded will.

PULSE 22

INTERROGATOR 4

WHAT WOMAN DO YOU WISH TO HAVE?
WHAT QUIET WARMTH? WHAT MATED SLEEP?
COMRADELY WHISPERING HANDS TO BATHE
YOUR SOUL IN PULSING MUSICS, FAR AND
    DEEP?
AFRICAN SAMSON, YOU LACK LOVE!

LOOKSMART AND WOMAN'S CROONING VOICE
Yes, soft and once again

I hear your voice
  Delilah calling;
    Drifting through blinded brain
      It promises
        New blissful feeling
          Delilah. . . .
            My delightful!
            Delilah . . . .
            Peaceful bride, cool
            Cool
            Togetherness
            Of all exploring
              Hands
            Will unlock us,
            Oh! free
            Cramped, muscled feeling
            In our little deaths
            In all our deathless
              Dust.

LOOKSMART

Dust sand dry desert Gaza
Dusty dusk over the sea
Where the paper dry South Easter
Day and duty blow away
Where my dust storms dry the Karroo
But the drought must also die
When love rains from my disaster
And when the spring grows gay.

And all this time must stop
When time will stay . . . .

INTERROGATOR 2

"GOD DIE BUKSEM IS BEDONNERD"
Ineffable and away

"HY'S STAPELGEK"

"SKOON VAN SY KOP"

"ALL RIGHT, OLD CHAP. CALL IT A DAY."

NARRATOR

Death may not be dishonor
Though it die, it die . . . . . . die day . . . . . .

LOOKSMART

Sweet death of day on kloof and bay;
Brave glowing rock and gleaming wave
Stay, distant light, I come but sway . . . .
Stay . . . . quiet . . . . pain . . . . or save me . . . wave . . . .

Stay distant, light; and eyeless, day!

My death is not dishonor's prey.

PULSE 23

NARRATOR AND LOOKSMART

Hands are not desperate that unlock
Imprisoned breath and fettered thought
Whose lonely echoing cell hollowly mock-
Ingly deride all that they, free, together, wrought.

LOOKSMART

Twin children have adopted love
And me to break the stammering walls
Of mourning, weeping, night:
A highstrung gemmed, frail woman's nerve

Streams telegrams of hope and calls
All men to morning's laughing light:

(WITH CHILDREN)
They call my name to manhood: "Looksmart,
Look smart in the eye." "Look smart, Looksmart."
And together: "Looksmart, Look!
We stand with you in the brave heart
Of casteless, castled time."

PULSE 24
NARRATOR
They took
His murder from the floor
And called a doctor: Closed the door.

The court must find that he has died.
Murder. Heart failure. Suicide.

PULSE 25
NARRATOR 1
What verdict coroners of time?

NARRATOR 2
What verdict coroners of the world
Will point this mischief's vilest crime
That has the heart's fine leaves hard-furled?

NARRATOR 1
Will antedate a tragic rhyme,
Fashion tongued love to chime, and chime
Changeless love's theme from clime to clime?—

NARRATOR 2
Passion that's star-flung, flame-pure, pearled!

Only your fisted anger now, sharp wrath,
Can blaze the trail of Looksmart's path
To passion beautied beyond death.
Love's antidote to poisoned time.

PULSE 26

NARRATOR 2

For when they draped
White shrouds around his raped
And brave but quiet heart,
No ghost escaped:
His spirit shaped
A song on the bloodless lips of dead Looksmart
On the smiling lips of his deathless heart:

PULSE 27

NARRATOR 1

Listen
This entire land
Bands brothers
Mother neighbors kin
In labors
All
Fire and joy

NARRATOR 2

And boy and girl
In spiral shell
And final pearl
Of bountiful
Growth
And beautiful
Fruit
Of truth

Through structure and stricture
And number and function
To nimble factor and facture
And section
And self
In life's wide flow
Waters graceful
Democracy
And fire
Beyond Distance
Of time and space
In starry
Knowledge
Throbs the race
Of living
Moving
Ocean
And
Animal
Man
Vegetable
Earth and motion
Man
And material
God is
Labor and love
In
Fashioning
Man
Finding
Him good
In the smile
Which we know is
Understanding

Beyond pain
And laughter
Beyond pleasure
And terror
And leisure
And beyond agony
Beyond
Ecstasy
Ecstasy
Which stands
Contemplative
Compassionate
Deedful
Needless
But for knowledge
And all love
And its sun
And its sum
Some life
Life that is lovely
While love moves and labor
And then ripeness is already
Another ripeness is all
All is ripeness
And silent singing
Nor is my rest
Your silence
For alone
Even alone
Oh alone
For alone
Social Man
Living Man
Loving, laboring smiling, rhythmical, muscular
Man

Your hungry spirits
Always hungry spirits
Yearning
Haunted me
Nor will leave you
Alone . . . .

The Potent Ash

THE POTENT ASH

by LEONARD KIBERA

This play, The Potent Ash *(which is also the title of the author's collection of short stories published by the East Africa Publishing House), won third prize in the BBC African Drama Contest, 1967, and was produced in London in June 1967, in the Africa Service of the BBC with the following cast:*

KARO . . . . *Cosmo Pieterse*

NARRATOR ⎫
WITCH DOCTOR ⎬ . . . . *Lionel Ngakane*

UNCLE ⎫
1ST VILLAGER ⎬ . . . . . *Bloke Modisane*

MALE VOICE 1 (GHOST) ⎫
2ND VILLAGER ⎬ . . *David Longdon*

MALE VOICE 2 (GHOST) ⎫
NAIMA ⎬ . . . *Louis Mahoney*

FEMALE VOICE (GHOST) . . . *Naomi Howe*

Note: This play is set in traditional Africa, locality undefined. The Characters should pronounce their words with a strong African accent to bring out this traditional flavor. The author would prefer the play to be continuous from beginning to end, but if an intermission is required (for the purpose of commercials, etc.) the producer should have it at the *******.

The play opens with three male and one female ghosts' voices calling, chanting, *Karo! Karo! Karo!!* in the howling wind. They are calling from a deep *Valley of the Dead and the Owls,* which means that echoes from the valley give the call a high-toned edge, a chilling effect. (The name of the condemned boy, Karo, has been deliberately chosen for its singsong quality when called out repeatedly.)

The howling wind and the calling voices then fade to the NARRATOR who appears only at the beginning, and reads with a deep, slow but deliberate voice. . . .

For the first time, the youth knew fear, dread of something strange and powerful. Unfelt and uncanny, like a myriad snakes in the dark approaching, but unapproachable. It was not just the fearfulness that stole into the imagination of boyhood flung into hostile loneliness by the tribe. This he had known two nights ago. He had then been afraid of what he could feel tangibly, something vulnerable like himself which he could see, grip, and fight. But this *was* fear, and he was not even running. There was nowhere to run; he could only submit. (*Up wind.*)

VOICES. Karo! Karo!! Karo!!! (*Karo moans, breathing hard. Fade to narrator.*)

NARRATOR. Karo staggered out of the darkness of his lone grass hut, into the darkness of the world outside. Hardly moving, he looked up. He could see nothing. His eyelids closed and pressed. A cloud of tears rolled out along the corners and he could now see the stars cast high and still in the vast night. They seemed to answer his silent plea with taunting winks, mocking and condemning him as everyone and everything were doing. He felt naked against the rushing wind for a goatskin was all he wore. He gathered it tighter around his waist. Then, he began his journey. . . . (*Up wind.*)

VOICES. Karo! Karo! Karo! (*Out voices, up wind only.*)

KARO. (*In a choked cry.*) I am Co-mi-ng! (*Slight echo, Coming coming!*)

MALE VOICE. Why do you not hurry?

KARO. The valley is too deep. It is too dark in the night. (*Up wind, three seconds.*)

VOICES. Karo, Karo, Karo!! (*Sound of Karo's feet skidding on dry, cracking leaves, bits.*)

KARO. I am falling! (*Cry, heavy noise of fall.*)

FEMALE VOICE. Karo!

KARO. I am coming!

FEM. VOICE. Why did you not come the first night we called? (*Up wind and fade to background.*) Answer!

KARO. I was afraid.

FEM. VOICE. Afraid? (*Cackles.*) Do you not want to meet your fathers now that they are dead and bodiless? Do you fear the ghosts of their bodies? (*Up wind, Karo moans, cry of an owl at a distance.*) Did we not call yesternight? Did I not call yesternight? (*Half-singing, monotonously.*) Karo—didn't your ancestor's voice defy the thunder and the rain—the whisper of the winds— *just* to reach you? Did it? Did we? (*Fading.*) Did I. . . .

KARO. You did . . . you did . . . please do not . . . (*Sound of fall, then another.*) (*To himself.*) I have fallen thrice. That is unlucky. (*Cry of an owl.*) And that cry of an owl—(*Voices call.*)

MALE VOICE. Karo, how old are you?

FEM. VOICE. He came to the tribe during the famine of the many. (*Chuckle.*) Barely a man but old enough to know better.

MALE VOICE. Old enough for blood to answer blood?

KARO. (*To himself.*) But I do not understand. I have been condemned in the Sacred Arena three days now. Is it because I do not belong to the tribe? My uncle told me one evening in his hut. . . .

(*Fade wind completely, disc effect for atmosphere.*)

OLD VOICE. Listen Karo. Watch out for malice. Malice against you, your adopted half-sisters and brothers of the clan.

KARO. Why?

OLD VOICE. No, no, do not speak. I know you do not understand. You know, Karo, (*sighs*) other boys have avoided you, refused to play with you. Why is your world confined to me and your mother? I know it will pain you, but. . . . This hut is getting too cold. Put some more firewood in the hearth and blow, I am too old. (*Sounds of dry sticks, some movement, and Karo blowing at the fire with his mouth.*) . . . I know it will pain you, but you are now old enough to know. Nara, my sister, is not your real mother. (*Appropriate noise and reaction from Karo.*) No, no, do not speak. One day I was grazing the cattle a long way from here. I left the cattle and went to drink some water at the river. I saw two women drop something several paces away. Then I heard them say—

FIRST WOMAN. No one has seen us.

SECOND WOMAN. Let us run away before someone does, you foolish woman.

They ran away and I saw they must have been from the

hostile tribe beyond the hills. I hastened to see what they had dropped. It was a child.

KARO. Me?

OLD VOICE. (*Not answering him.*) Maybe you had been born a twin and you were the unfortunate one to be cast away. Maybe your mother was a young unmarried girl, a shame to her clan by your birth. I could not tell. But I took you to my sister Nara who could never have a child of her own.

KARO. Is that why they mock her?

OLD VOICE. Yes. (*Sighing.*) She has had a hard time, Nara. She has been the laughing stock of other women and that is why she loves you so much. She approached the medicine men so that your being from another tribe could be cleansed. It did not matter that you were only a baby; you had to be cleansed. But the medicine men refused. They all said—

WITCH DOCTOR. What? (*Slowly as if quite self-satisfied.*) I could never risk severing the chain of fate which blesses my trade by attempting to cleanse the blood of another tribe! That child is impossible and not of our temper. I cannot burn out with the smoke of the ram on the furnace under the fig-tree, the dark, destructive fire glowing within him. (*Intimately.*) Be—Because—even after the devil within him has burnt to ashes, there will remain not cold and powerless ash, but ash that revives its malice. Like the ash that lies so cold and dead in the hearth and yet when we use it in food for flavor, it comes alive in the mouth with a taste that is salty, almost pungent. Potent Ash that in sickly wind blows unseen, unannounced, like a shadow creeping everywhere, into everything. Our tribe will suspect that child with every cow that dies, with every period of drought, like the ill wind that in dry weather carries destructive ravaging fire from hut to hut. (*Fading.*) No—do not ask me to help . . . do not . . .

OLD VOICE. That is why, Karo, they warn their children to avoid you. Stop crying! I am old and I had to tell you now before I am dead. Nara could never bring herself to tell you. (*Up wind, disc effect for initial atmosphere.*)

KARO. (*To himself.*) Yes, I was old enough to know. Now my uncle is dead. He was the only one who understood.***

VOICES. Karo! Karo!! Karo!!!

KARO. I am coming!

MALE VOICE. Listen, do you know the voice speaking to you?

MALE VOICE. Answer!

KARO. No.

MALE VOICE. No? Why is the Potent Ash condemned to the Sacred Arena where only the wind may step?

KARO. I killed a man, I killed . . . Naima . . . I did not mean. . . .

MALE VOICE. Why may no one come near the Ash except in this valley of the forefathers?

KARO. Because I killed . . . Killed . . . Killed! (*Sound of his fist hitting furiously against something.*)

MALE VOICE. Why did you kill *me?*

KARO. (*To himself.*) This cannot be Naima. But is he not a spirit now? Or is it Naima's clan come to avenge him?

MALE VOICE. Do you hit a man when he is down? You sent me amongst the ancestors before my time!

KARO. I did not mean to. I was lonely. I only wanted to play at wrestling but you fetched a quarrel. (*To himself.*) It was the day of sacrifice. The whole village had assembled at the fig-tree so that we could all pray to the gods for rain and rich harvest. Then, after the sacrifice, I saw him. I shouted—(*Disc effect for atmosphere: noise from a crowd dispersing, etc.*)

KARO. Ah, Naima, there you are. I need company. Shall I walk to your father's hut with you?

NAIMA. Why should you walk home with me? We did not come together. I want to join my friend Mago. We are going wrestling in our compound.

KARO. Ah, let me come and wrestle with you as well.

NAIMA. You dare let your shadow stray into my father's compound and the Village Elders will hear about it. We shall finish you!

KARO. But why are you so cold? I do not want to stay at our hut day after day, full moon after full moon, season after season. I—(*almost lightheartdly*) I am not a woman, Naima. I want to go grazing cattle or hunting (*intimately*) those little virgin daughters of mean women with my riika! (*Urging.*) Oh, come on, let us see who can knock the other down. I will wrestle your life out with all those people to see! And then your father will laugh at you for the rest of the new moon. Come on!

NAIMA. Keep your hands away from me. (*Pause: then begins to tease, singing.*) Potent Ash, Potent Ash, play—play, Potent Ash, but do go home and play there. . . .

KARO. Why do you call me that? (*Rough movement.*) I only asked to play, like friends.

NAIMA. Leave me alone. (*Heavy sound—single—of punching.*)

KARO. You dare hit me? Call me that again!

NAIMA. I will!

KARO. You do!

NAIMA. Potent—(*Timely heavy punch from Karo.*)

KARO. I'll kill you, I'll kill you! (*Screams, cry, curses.*)

NAIMA. He is killing me. Do not let him use that—Help!

FIRST MAN. (*Distantly.*) Who is that crying over there? You, stop it, you!

SECOND MAN. It is that Shadow of the Night! He is

hitting the son of Kara. Stop his evil arm! (*Scream, more voices close up.*) He has killed him!

FIRST MAN. Catch him there. You there, catch him (*cries of who—where—who*)—the Devil's wing, you fools. He is running away. (*Appropriate noises and sounds.*) He is escaping into the Sacred Arena. (*Pandemonium.*)

A WOMAN. He has entered the shrub of the Sacred Arena. Now we cannot get him. The gods will be upon us. We cannot have any rain. (*Curses, general uproar.*)

FIRST MAN. Summon his clan and the Elders. I knew it would happen before the moon was out. He had become very aggressive. Malice like that cannot wait for the moon to wane. (*Fading.*) It was just a matter of time. . . . (*Disc effect: initial atmosphere, up wind, voices.*)

VOICES. Karo! Karo!! Karo!!!

KARO. I am coming.

MALE VOICE. Why did you continue to hit and pound even after I lay unconscious?

KARO. I had no bitterness toward you. (*Very slowly to himself.*) But it made me strangely happy. It was as if in trodding Naima into the mud I had triumphed over a cruel people who the gods had imposed upon me, but who always said I had been imposed upon them. I had released through each blow the foam of inhibited bitterness bubbling within me. My uncle had told me to use my shield, always to defend myself. But—

FEMALE VOICE. —you hit deep with your arrow. Now your triumph is your curse. The bee has hit once and cannot sting again. If you were not guilty, why did you choose to flee into the Sacred Arena? Now the gods are angry!

KARO. I had to run away, anywhere. (*Up wind.*)

VOICES. Karokarokaro!

MALE VOICE. I repeat, do you hit a man when he is down?

Karo. You attacked me first. If I had let you up again you would have killed me.

Male Voice. Blundering calabash! (*Sound of Karo's feet, moans.*) Do you know what an evil spell you have cast upon the clan?

Karo. I know I have done them wrong.

Male Voice. Wrong! Be damned. Nara is dead.

Karo. Dead, mother dead?

Female Voice. The goats and cattle of the clan have been stolen and your clan is impoverished. They hate you. Your aunt has had twins which the clan cast away after your spell this morning. Why do you stop?

Karo. Why do you kill me this way, call me every night. . . . I want to explain.

Voices. (*Commanding.*) You will come here! (*Echo, sound of Karo's feet on cracking leaves, etc. Silence except for howling wind, lasting not less than 20 seconds.*)

Second Male Voice. (*Deep, near, husky.*) Here—here —give me your hand, here! (*Movement, moans, resistance, etc.*) Let us go into the cave of your forefathers! (*Stop howling wind. We hear them join more voices in the cave. Disc effect for atmosphere.*)

Voices. (*Simultaneously.*) Here no one will know.

> (*At this point the producer can, discreetly, introduce a drum which sounds more like the beat of the heart, at intervals of one second. It should draw into a crescendo at the end.*)

Karo. (*Hysterically.*) You are no ghosts. Is that not you Erabe? You pretended to be Naima. Why is my clan killing me? (*Rough handling.*) Ghosts have no shape. . . . You killed Nara!

Voices. You and your mother have brought us enough evil. Your blood and ours be forever apart! (*Last scream.*)

DANCE

Les Ballets
Africains Sont Beaux

GUINEA'S NATIONAL ENSEMBLE
IN SAN FRANCISCO

by JOSEPH OKPAKU [1]

Consumed by their own energies, the spent winds retire to the distant hills. The angry waves, placated by the sacrificial worship of a frothful turbulence, slowly retreat back to sea, calm, enchanting, and no less elegant in their soothing pacific sigh than in the roaring thunder of their earth-shaking advance.

And somewhere, deep in the midst of the crowd, a transitory moan escapes a heart that for too long has been disciplined to stifle the no less than human urge to yield her subtle sensibilities to the sublime experience of letting go in answer to the magic call of the rhythms of drums and the heart-rending tunes of human voices.

[1] Reprinted with permission from *The Stanford Daily,* Stanford University, February 1, 1968.

Such is the mood of the tropical African storm, at midnight. Such was the mood evoked at the Curran Theater in San Francisco on January 30, 1968.

And like the almost audible and palpable calm that succeeds the awe-inspiring thunderstorm (having come, it seems, to deliver the new-born day safely into the delicate arms of the African Dawn), Bakary Sissoko took over the stage from his agile, acrobatic colleagues, and to the self-accompaniment of his thirty-stringed cora, serenaded the motley audience to a trance that was a most fitting compliment to the talent of the artist.

It was no less fitting that his solos were backed by a chorus of elegantly attired maidens who swayed with grace, flirted with innocent charm, and teased the group with a certain touch of artistic purity.

Elegant was the ballad; elegant the movement. And the singing was reminiscent of the homophony or gallant style of the early postbaroque era, and the beginnings of the Age of Elegance.

The African ballet, the National Ensemble of the Republic of Guinea, is the twenty-year-old brainchild of poet-politician Keita Fodeba.

The group of about forty young men and women, some of the ladies being certainly in their teens, is a dance drama ensemble which creates its own definition.

Gifted as much with agility as with flowing grace, the troupe fuses the power and force of its leaping and somersaulting male dancers with the poignant rococo of the songs and movements of their female counterparts.

The evening's program opened with a dance to Kakilambe, the Goddess of the people of Baga. This was a rich dance ritual in plea for prosperity and fertility.

> *O! Nimba! Goddess of Fertility*
> *O! Nimba! Thou who brings*
> *forth fruit from the dust.*

[204]

> *Here are my breasts. May they*
> *be as big as yours.*

Then followed a surrealistic fetish pantomime, the-
matically akin to scenes of torment in medieval drama,
in which all the deities of the forest, guardians of public
morality—from the little blood-thirsty "Wononleaguis"
to the towering, imposing, awe-inspiring stilt masquerades—sadistically torture a pair of young lovers for
daring to trespass forbidden land—figuratively.

Dramatic, aesthetic and perhaps emotional relief is
brought by the ballad of the griot, singing amongst
others:

> *Do not cry, Son of the Country.*
> *See, when you cry, the whole country cries—*
> *See when you smile, all the country smiles—*
> *Guinea will find her destiny by her own will*
> *   and according to her wishes.*
> *Only those who have no faith doubt this,*
> *   but their doubts are without foundation. . .*

a subtle prelude to the political indictment of the next
and major feature of the evening, the dance-dramatiza-
tion of Keita Fodeba's poetic understatement, *Midnight.*

MIDNIGHT!	*For the tender heart which listens and understands, all sing Midnight.*
MIDNIGHT!	*It is the naive monotonous lullaby of the nurse lulling her child.*
MIDNIGHT!	*It is the complaint of her lover who, in the calm of the nights, asks favors from his beloved.*
MIDNIGHT!	*It is the sad song of the bird in the branches, the despairing sob of the witch doctor hard-pressed by the severe*

gods; it is the thunder which growls in the distance.

MIDNIGHT! *It is all that sobs, all that cries, for Midnight is also the tragedy of Manding.*

This is the plain but sad evocation of a real happening which took place in Siguiri (Upper Guinea).

Using the commonest theme, that of young lovers, Fodeba makes the subtlest and most incisive cut yet at the overlords of Africa's colonial past and present.

Two young lovers. The elders approve. An official feels otherwise. Of course. And barely halfway through the wedding festivities, the official, in a costume strikingly unlike that of the rest of the cast, rudely intrudes with a pair of obviously African local constables.

The would-be bridegroom is taken away and tortured to death, to the noble indignation but tactical impotence of the people, who cannot hold their machetes against the power of gunpowder—and are too wise (?) to take a chance.

But whether or not an American audience which can cast a white man if it wants, and a Negro if it cares to, got the connection between the action and the costume of the official—a recognition most crucial to the entire drama—is another question.

My guess is that it did not; for if it had, it would have applauded differently—with a little remorse, perhaps? For the official, though apparently African, wore *white* dress, designed not like the robes and loin cloths of the rest but in a Western military fashion.

He was a white man, the epitome of the colonial master. Amusingly, though, it was obvious from his physical features that he was African.

The juxtaposition of this and the Forest episode is not accidental. The meaning of the whole drama exists on such multiple levels of profundity that to attempt to analyze them, even sketchily, in the limited space of a newspaper critique, is to do gross injustice to the essence of the work itself.

Suffice it, therefore, to say that the unique dramatic experience provided a window, in its modest way, to the rich culture and bubbling vitality of Human Culture beyond the confines of the limited Western experience.

To this end the drama might have been taken out into the streets and the squares as it was meant to be presented.

Then, and perhaps only then—with the audience in the streets or in horse-shoe formation, forming part of the song-and-dance chorus, and the stilt masquerades towering twenty or more feet above the upward-gazing crowd—will the full awe, grandeur and power be given full scope to draw the audience's soul up towards itself, infusing and soothing it with the grace and delicacy of its more sublime qualities.

As it is, the fourth wall stage, with its protective proscenium, is an inadequate setting for this type of drama.

PROFILES

of

AFRICAN

ARTISTS

Jean Ikelle-Matiba

by PAULETTE J. TROUT

Jean Ikelle-Matiba, one of the most versatile and gifted of the new generation of French-speaking African writers, was born in Song-Ndong, Cameroun, on April 26, 1936. He studied law in Paris and since 1963 has resided in West Germany. The author of several essays on African politics, Matiba has contributed to the German review *Aeropag,* to *Présence Africaine,* and to the *Journal of Modern African Studies.* He is also the official representative of *Présence Africaine* in Germany, and has lectured widely throughout Europe for the Society of African Culture.

But Matiba's greatest acclaim has come as a novelist. In 1963, he received the coveted *Grand Prix de l'Afrique Noire* for his novel *Cette Afrique-là* (Paris: *Présence Africaine*). The *Grand Prix* is awarded annually in Paris for the best literary work in French on a non-European subject. Earlier winners of the prize had been the Ivoirian novelist Aké Loba for *Kocumbo, l'étudiant noir* (Paris: Flammarion, 1960), and Cheikh Hamidou Kane of Senegal for his semi-autobiographical *L'Aventure ambigue* (Paris: Julliard; translated into English as *Ambiguous Adventure,* and published by Walker and Company, New York).

Matiba's prize-winning novel, though not yet available in English, has been translated into German and has received critical acclaim in Europe. *Cette Afrique-là* is the first volume of a planned trilogy, to be followed by works entitled *Transition* and *La Solitude.*

Essayist, lecturer, novelist, Jean Ikelle-Matiba makes his first appearance in our pages as a poet.[1] His vein is highly cosmopolitan as he reflects about the European places where his travels have taken him, and captures the individuality of each of the locales.

Yet, like so many African poets before him, Matiba likes to contrast the coldness and artificiality of Europe with the warmth and naturalness of his homeland. But he is by no means uncritical of Africa, and, like Senghor and Dadié, seems disillusioned at the changes and social disintegration taking place there.

The simplicity of tone of many of Matiba's poems reminds one of the medieval French poet Charles d'Orléans. The theme of travel echoes Baudelaire, and his short, melancholy verse brings to mind the work of Paul Verlaine. Matiba admits that he has been influenced by these writers. Among Negro authors, he particularly admires the force of Césaire, the spirit of reconciliation he finds in Senghor, and the traditionalism of Birago Diop.

Matiba seems to possess all the qualifications necessary to take up where Senghor, Birago Diop, Bernard Dadié,

[1] The poems appear on pages 85–97.

David Diop, and the other French African poets of liberation have left off. The literature of protest has played its role in the emergence of independent Africa. Perhaps Matiba can be, for his African readers and for a wider public, a new voice of inspiration.

David Diop: Negritude's Angry Young Man

by PAULETTE J. TROUT
AND ELLEN CONROY KENNEDY

David Diop's literary career began while he was still a student at the Lycée Marcelin Berthelot near Paris, in the late 1940's. His teacher, Léopold Sédar Senghor, was impressed with the youngster's "original inner life" and selected several early poems for inclusion in the history-making *Anthologie de la nouvelle poésie nègre et malgache* (1948), which Jean-Paul Sartre prefaced with the famous essay "Black Orpheus." Later, David Diop contributed to *Présence Africaine,* the cultural review of the Negro world edited in Paris, and participated in the Negro Writers and Artists Conference in Paris (1956) and Rome (1960). *Coups de Pilon,* his single slim book of seventeen poems, was published by Editions Présence Africaine in 1956.

The poet was born in 1927, in Bordeaux, where his

father happened to be teaching school. By virtue of being born in Dakar, David's father was a French citizen. He had met and married a young widow from the Cameroons while serving in the French army. Though they lived intermittently in Senegal, David spent most of his life in France. The family was Christian, and in many respects assimilated, but took great pride in their African heritage. Eventually widowed for a second time, David's mother managed somehow to raise and educate her five children in wartime France. Today, David's brother is a surgeon in Dakar, his youngest sister is married to a pharmacist in Thiès, another is one of Senegal's three women judges, and a third, the eldest, is married to Alioune Diop, founder and editor of *Présence Africaine*. David himself completed the demanding studies for two *baccalauréats* and the *licence-ès-lettres* despite months and years in sanatoriums with a recurrent illness that plagued him from childhood.

Returning to Senegal in the late 1950's, he taught for a year at the Lycée Maurice Delafosse in Dakar. His home there quickly became a meeting place for young intellectuals. In 1958, Diop was named principal of a secondary school at Kindia in Guinea. Two years later, the thirty-three-year-old writer was returning with his wife from a vacation in France when both were killed in an airplane crash near Dakar, leaving their five small children orphaned.

Until his untimely death, David Diop was emerging as a leader of the younger generation of "Negritude" writers, those who reached their twenties in the postwar years. Many of his poems take up images, themes, and accents already introduced by such older French-speaking West Indians in the Negritude school as Jacques Roumain and Léon Damas. The influence of Aimé Césaire on David Diop's work is especially strong. While the younger poet's gifts cannot be compared with Césaire's, his work has a distinct personal stamp that stems from its directness, simplicity, and raw emotional power. The impact of every line, every word, is intentional. The angry young man meant his poems to "burst the eardrums of those who do not wish to hear them." *Coups de pilon* refers of course to pounding or grinding with a pestle, the commonest method in Africa of preparing many foods. Gerald Moore has suggested "Pounding" as an English equivalent for the forceful image of the French title. We suggest "Hammerblows" as another.

David Diop's militance has been well represented in recent anthologies. Most of his poems are essentially indictments, sometimes also calls to arms, urgent statements in images and rhythm of pain, indignation, accusation, exhortation. "The Vultures," "A Time of Martyrdom," and "The Renegade" are three examples in this vein. Another example, which has not to our knowledge been translated before, is "To a Black Child." The incident that inspired this poem is the 1955 lynching in Mississippi of a Chicago youngster named Emmet Till. David Diop had not been to America, but like nearly all Africans and West Indians in the Negritude movement, he identified closely with the American Negro. He was deeply shocked by the Till affair, and by the fact that the murderers, though known, were acquitted in a trial that made a mockery of justice.

"Negro Tramp," dedicated to Aimé Césaire, and inspired by the pathetic old man the narrator encounters in Césaire's *Cahier d'un retour au pays natal* ("Notes on a return to the native land"), and the memorable "Africa" are two of Diop's finest achievements. They transcend the polemic with the ardor of a poetic vision that goes further to affirm and celebrate: ". . . . I am sharpening a hurricane to plough the future with . . ." "To My Mother," "With You," "Rama Kam," and "Times" are less typical David Diop poems, that attest to a greater range of sensibility than the poet is usually given credit for.

Léopold Sédar Senghor had hoped to see his young countryman's talent mature, his bitterness and anger soften with understanding and compassion. It was President Senghor who pronounced the funeral oration in Dakar, recalling David's courage during the "long calvary" of his youth, the months and years of sickness. These and more purely psychic anguishes, David Diop has recorded in a series of lucid images: "ragged days with a narcotic taste," "anxious hangings on the edge of cliffs," and "sleep inhabited by alcohol," together with a love that brought "necklaces of laughter," his second marriage. "Through your long hospital nights," said President Senghor, "you identified with your crucified people. Your sufferings became their sufferings; your anguish, their anguish; your hope, their hope." Senghor's words were a generous tribute to a voice he found "hard and black as basalt," a voice destined never to reach maturity, but which sang ardently and unforgettably of "Africa my Africa."

Alirwana Mugalula Mukiibi

by LAURA DAVIDSON

"To me art has developed in the course of time from a pastime into a passion and consequently into a profession. My entire joy in life hangs on the brushes' tip." Thus speaks one of Uganda's most appealing, and articulate, young artists. Alirwana Mugalula Mukiibi, born in 1943 at Kira Village in Buganda, is the seventh son of a former school teacher turned farmer, whose main ambition was to see his children well educated. Of his father, Alirwana remarks, "He was never lenient with a child lazy about education." Yet it was his father who always encouraged his son's art.

"I used to make some naive drawings on the walls of my father's house, using charcoal from my mother's

---

1 Photographs of Mr. Mukiibi's drawings and paintings are shown on pages 220 to 225 and of his sculpture on the frontispiece.

fireplace and raw banana which, when it dries, leaves a white chalky impression on the mud walls. Then I started drawing with coloured pencils, and used to, with gum from a nearby gum tree, stick the drawings onto the walls of my father's sitting room. He appreciated my works of art and my artistic activities, so much so that my father assigned me the corridor as my permament 'gallery.'

"My father's house is a very old one and the walls are made out of mud and wattle which naturally develops cracks. These cracks form a labyrinth-like pattern which would inspire me whenever I looked at it. I tried to figure out human forms, animal forms and so on."

Of course it was not only his parents who aided the young artist. He thinks also of Mr. Hannington Matoru and Mr. John Kisaka, early art teachers, and of his friend, Dr. F. J. Bennett, who took the accompanying photographs. One must also consider Alirwana's formal training in art.

"After my primary education at Kira Primary School, I was lucky to join King's College Buddo, one of the few secondary schools in Uganda where art was taught as a subject in the curriculum at that time." Of this period he recalls, "I used to read about artists all over the world and I came to admire their life characters, their behaviour and their humble position in the society they lived in. These characteristics suited my nature and ambitions for I naturally love to be but in the background of society and never in front."

As his studies and interest in art grew, he made the decision to pursue a career in art. "After the completion of my senior secondary studies in 1962, I applied for admission to the Makerere University College School of Fine Arts, in spite of discouragement from a number of my friends and some of my relatives. Fortunately I managed to satisfy the requirements to the art school.

[219]

MUKIIBI
Busy (Making Basket), 1966, oil, 24 x 27½ inches

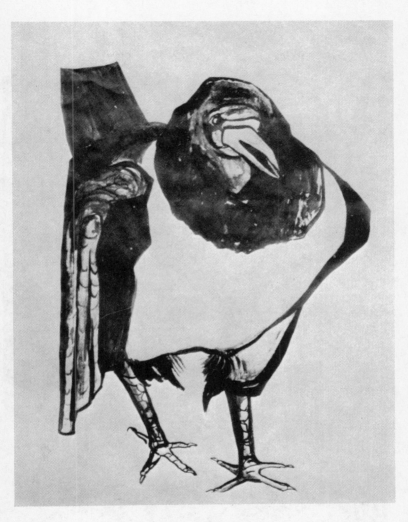

MUKIIBI
Crow, ink drawing, 1½ x 2 feet

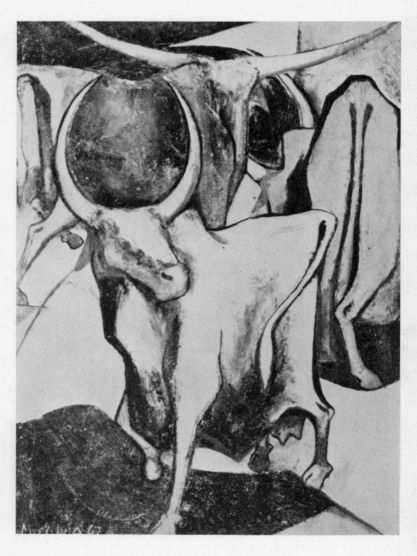

MUKIIBI
Cows, 1967, oil, 23 x 30½ inches

MUKIIBI
Three Dar es Salaam Women, oil, 3¼ x 26 inches

MUKIIBI
Evening Talk, oil, 22 x 33 inches
(Collection Mr. Robins, London)

MUKIIBI
Home-bound, oil, 26 x 20 inches
(Collection Dr. F. I. Bennett, Makerere University College)

There, I practised in all the branches of art offered: painting, sculpture, graphics, designing and pottery. My chief branch was painting, although at times I fail to hit the balance as to whether I am more of a painter than a sculptor or vice versa.

"In March of 1967 I graduated with a first class award and won the Art School's annual academic prize in painting. After graduation I voluntarily went to an up-country school to teach art for some three months, during which time I executed many paintings and drawings. Upon returning to Kampala, I put up my first one-man show in August 1967 in the Nommo Gallery, Kampala, Uganda. The show earned me much praise, relatively, and thus of course, encouragement."

Treating the question of how he actually works, Alirwana replies, "I am always at the easel painting or sketching. For me there is nothing like waiting until I am in the mood, as people normally excuse themselves. It is oneself who controls the mood! Once at work, the mood automatically comes. To me, to work daily is instinctive. Seldom does a day pass without my doing some artistic work. At present I mainly work in oils, on sized hard-boards. I work at any time of the day and at times I can work until very late into the night."

Then, reflecting upon his art, Alirwana observes, "I would call my present movement in art a semi-realistic one, conditioned by the time and circumstances. I believe that a work of art is but an expression of the artist's mind about a circumstance. A style is a by-product of practising. Having a style in mind would, so to speak, sound a note of 'putting the cart before the horse.' It happens that I may plan a work, but upon execution it comes out spontaneously—the result being different from the original plan. In my works I make sure that the mood of an instance is evoked. A painting must convey the mood it typifies. A balanced design is always

[226]

rendered by linear and curvilinear reinforcements which occur in most of my works. My painting minus its colour will render a balanced design, devoid of any lamentable symmetry."

As to whether he has been influenced by other artists, he comments, "Degas, Pollock, Calder, Toulouse Lautrec and Daumier are some of the masters I would mention at any time if we were talking art. But when I am working, or when I sit down to work, I never have in mind that I will paint like Degas or Rubens, although of course an inspiration could naturally filter through."

Continuing the discussion of his art while considering it in relation to society he says:

"My paintings are, so to speak, sort of key-hole impressions of the society. Comprehensive subjects, like peasant family groups, used to dominate my works. But when in 1965 I visited Dar es Salaam, my work at the coast took on another format. Last year when I stayed in a place foreign to me, I used to look at life from 'quite far,' for we had no communicating language so as to mix entirely with the society and the result was my painting landscapes with people. I treated the figures as but silhouettes in the enchanting background with the hot climate giving a mirage-like impression. Human figures, cattle, animals and birds in general dominate my works. In sculpture especially, bird and animal forms really dominate.

"In 1966/67 I wrote an academic thesis on 'The Clans and Totems of the Baganda.' I did many paintings of the animals and birds which occur in the totemic system of the people—the Baganda. I sculpted some of them and also did many etchings of the totemic symbols. Our folklore is deeply embedded in most of my works."

Exactly because Alirwana is so profoundly a part of his society, he cannot in any way separate his art from the needs of his country. On this topic of the artist in society he has some very definite opinions. "My people have not yet come to know the value of art in our society. It is our duty as artists to help them to achieve this. But we cannot achieve it overnight. Time will play a great role. That is why I decided to teach art in secondary schools, to the young generations, for 'their knowing the value of art' will be transmitted to the society. I have to share my talent with others."

However, Alirwana does not intend to teach for so very long as he hopes to continue his own growth by travelling and acquiring a greater knowledge of the skills and techniques in evidence elsewhere. Eventually, he intends to find the time and money to settle down to work in his own studio, for it is there that he can create and derive his own pleasure from art.

BIBLIOGRAPHY

A Supplement to Janheinz Jahn's Bibliography of Neo-African Literature: Africa, America, and the Caribbean

by PAUL PARICSY

Janheinz Jahn's bibliography, "*Die neoafrikanische Literatur. Gesamtbibliographie von den Anfangen bis zur Gegenwart,*" came out in 1965 at Köln, and in English in 1965, at London.

The work of the widely known German historian of literature J. Jahn gives an extensive view of Neo-African literature. The exact bibliographical data, the translations of the titles of literary works written in whichever African language, the ascertainment of the genre, the precise collection of those works which are published also in translation, all these make his bibliography a very authentic source book for all those interested in African literature.

The following is a supplement to this bibliography. All the items below belong to that part of Jahn's book which deals with the works of continental African writers.

The bibliography is divided into two different parts: 1. anthologies; 2. works. The entries are in alphabetical order.

The bibliography consists of seven anthologies and one hundred and fifty-two works of one hundred and fifteen writers. This number includes fifty-three works by forty-four writers who are not mentioned in J. Jahn's Bibliography. Furthermore, there are sixty-four hitherto unknown works and thirty-five newer editions or translations of works by writers whose names also appear in J. Jahn's Bibliography.

The bibliographical signs and abbreviations used here are the same as those applied by Jahn. Besides the names of the writers we have included their native country and the language in which the work is written if it is not a European language. We were not in a position to provide the translation of the titles of the works. We have also ascertained the genre of the works. We have applied the following symbols in addition to the abbreviations used by J. Jahn.

* before the writer's name: means the writer was not mentioned in Jahn's Bibliography.

before the title of the work: means a work which was not mentioned in Jahn's work.

ad 217 before the title of the work: here, 217, for example, is either a newer edition or translation of such a work, which is to be found in the work of J. Jahn under the same number.

first name in italics: The first name or a part of first name, which is not in Jahn's Bibliography.

For collections, I used as source books the following:

Nigerian Publications, Ibadan: Ibadan University Press 1959-1965.

South African National Bibliography, Pretoria: State Library 1959-1965.

Index Translationum. Repertoire International des Traductions. Vol 17. Paris: UNESCO 1966.

Schöne Schriften aus Afrika. Bonn: Deutsche Africa-Gesellschaft 1962.

In addition, some thirty-five anthologies of African literature were consulted.

ANTHOLOGIES

BENNIE, William Govan, ed.
ad 756 Imibengo, Xhosa, 2nd ed. Lovedale, South Africa: Lovedale Press 1960. 276 p. Nars & Lyr.

BOOYSEN, Charles Murray, ed.
Tales of South Africa: an anthology of South African short stories. Cape Town: Timmins 1963. 220 p. Nars.

HARDER, Uffe, ed. & tr.
ad 16 Moderne afrikansk digtning. Kobenhavn: Borgen 1962. 143 p. Borgens Billigborger 9. Lyr.

MACNAB, Roy Martin
South African poetry: a new anthology. Eds: Roy Martin Macnab & C. Gulston. London: Collins 1948. Lyr.

MARGARIDO, Alfredo, ed.
Poetas de Mocambique. Lisboa: Casa dos Estudantes do Império 1962. Lyr.

MAMBO LEO: Mashairi ya Mambo Leo. Swahili. Poems from the Swahili newspaper "Mambo Leo." Selected by the Inter-territorial Language Committee. 2 vols. 2nd ed. London: Sheldon Press 1955-1962. Lyr.

NEVES, João Alves das
Poetas e contistas africanos de expressão portuguesa, Capo Verde, Quine, São Tomé e Principe, Angola, Mocambique.

[233]

Ed. & Tr., João Alves das Neves. São Paulo, Brasil: Editora Brasiliense 1963. 211 p. Lyr & Nars.

WORKS

ABUBAKAR, Imam. Nigeria.
\# Tarihin annabi Muhammadu. Hausa. Zaria, Nigeria: Gaskiya corporation 1960. 73 p.

ACHEBE, Chinua *Albert*. Nigeria.
ad 78 do sln: Okonkvo. Tr: Branko Avsenak. Maribor: Zalozba Obzorja 1964. 160 p. Ro.
ad 82 do mag: Örökké nyugtalanul. Tr: Mária Borbás. Budapest: Európa 1964. 214 p. Ro.

ACQUAAH, Gaddiel Robert. Ghana.
\# The morning after. London: Goodwin 1961. Ro.

AJAO, Aderogba. Nigeria.
ad 97 do esp: A espaldas del tigre. Tr: Mireya Noriega. México, Mexico: F. Trillas 1964. ANar.
ad 97 do jap: Dattô; Africajin kyôsan tôin no shuki. Tr: Nishino Terutarô. Tokyo: Jiji tsùshinsha 1964. 245 p. ANar.

*AKAR, John J. Sierra Leone.
Cry Tamba. MS Th. *West African Review,* July 1954. London 1954.

*AKUNEME, D. Nkem. Nigeria.
Elekere Agso: the quack doctor. Awo-Omamma, Nigeria: Aut 1964. 72 p. Ro.

ALMEIDA, Santos, José de. Angola.
\# Servidão de mulher, episódios provincianos. São Paulo, Brasil: Editora Brasiliense 1947. 211 p. ill. Ro.
\# Viagem à Itália. São Paulo, Brasil: Editora Brasiliense 1949. 251 p. Itin.

AMON D'ABY, Francois Joseph Koutoua. Ivory Coast.
\# Krack part à Bangui, drame en 3 actes. Paris: Éd. du Scorpion 1959. 128 p. Th.

BÂ, Ahmadou Hampaté. Mali.
\# Koumen; texte initatique des pasteurs peul par A.H. Bâ et G. Dieterlen. Paris: Mouton 1961. 65 p. École pratique des hautes études, Sorbonne, VIe section 1. Mo.

BALOGUN, Kolawole. Nigeria.

\# Mission to Ghana; memoir of a diplomat. New York: Vantage press 1963. 79 p. ANar.

*BABOLOLA, S. Adeboye. Nigeria.

Iká k'Oníkà. Yoruba. Adaptation of Shakespeare's The Merchant of Venice in prose. Ibadan, Nigeria: Western Region Literature Committee 1954. Nar.

BETI, Mongo, i.e., Alexandre Biyidi; Pseud: Eza Boto & Mongo Beti. Cameroun.

ad 157 do liet: Misija beigusies. Tr: Milda Grinfelde. Riga: Lat-gos-izdat 1964. 193 p. Ro.

ad 155 do ce: Chudák Kristuspán z Bomby. Tr: Ludek Kárl. Praha: Státnī nakladatelstvī krasné literatury, hudby a umeni 1964. 237 p. Ro.

ad 157 do rom: Misiune îndeplinitâ. Tr: Livia Storescu. Bucuresti; Ed. tineretului 1964. 192 p. Ro.

BOLAMBA, Antoine-Roger. Congo.

\# Premiers essais. Elisabethville: Ed. de l'Essor du Congo 1947.

*CARDOSA, Antonio. Angola.

Poemas de circunstancia. Lisboa: Edicao da Casa dos estudantes do Império 1953. Lyr.

*CHIFAMBA, Jane. South Africa.

Ngano dzepasi chigare. Shona, Cape Town: Oxford University Press in assoc. with the Southern Rhodesia Literature Bureau 1964. III, 60 p. ill. Nar.

*CHIVAURA, B.M.

Madetembedzo. . .

vid. Shamuyarira, M.

CLARK, John Pepper. Nigeria.

\# Three plays. Song of a goat. The Masquerade. The raft. London: Oxford University Press 1964. 134 p. Three crowns books. Th.

DANA, Minazana. South Africa.

ad 857 Kufundwa ngamava. Xhosa. 2nd ed. Cape Town: Oxford University Press 1963. III, 98 p.

DANQUAH, Joseph Boakye. Ghana.

\# Liberty, a page from the life of J. B. Danquah. Accra, Ghana: H.K. Akyempong 1960. 34 p. ANAR.

* DAVIES, Hezekiah Olufɛla. Nigeria.

The Victor Olaiya story. Lagos, Nigeria: Aut. 1964. 52 p. ill. B.

*DE GRAFT, J.C. Ghana.

Sons and daughters. London: Oxford University Press 1964. 54 p. Three crowns books. Ro.

DHLAMINI, Seth *Zondeleleni Selby*. South Africa.

ad 858 Itshe lesivivane. Zulu, Johannesburg: Afrikaanse Pers-Boekhandel 1961. 60 p. Lyr.

DHLOMO, Rolfes Reginald Raymond. South Africa.

ad 867 UNomalanga ka Ndengezi. Zulu. 2nd ed. Pietermaritzburg: Shuter & Shooter 1964. VI, 113 p. Ro.

*DOLAMO, Elon Ramarisane. Lesotho.

Mahlale. Motho ke leobu o fetola mebala. Pedi. Johnnesburg: Afrikaanse Pers-Boekhandel 1961. 89 p. Nar.

Mononi. Pedi. Pretoria, South Africa: Van Schaik 1962. 112 p. Nars.

Ithute go reta. Pedi. Johannesburg: Afrikaanse Pers-Boekhandel 1962. 45 p. Lyr.

EASMON, *Raymond* Sarif. Sierra Leone.

ad 244 Dear parent and ogre. London: Oxford University Press 1964. 107 p. Three crowns books. Th.

*EDYANG, Ernest. Nigeria.

Emotan of Benin. A play in three acts. *Nigeria Magazine* No. 76. Lagos, Nigeria. March 1963. Th.

*EGBUJIOBI, Pius Muorokwu. Nigeria.

A wife from Bright Street. Orlu, Nigeria: Aut. 1964. 45 p. Nar.

EQUIANO, Olaudah. Nigeria.

ad 278 do sve: Berättelsen om Olaudah Equiano eller Gustavus Vasa, afrikanen. Tr: Kjell Ekström. Stockholm: Tiden 1964. 219 p. A.

FILHO, Ernesto Lara. *vid.* Lara, Ernesto Pires Barreto de

FODEBA, Keita. Guinée.

Keita Fodeba & Michel Huet: Les hommes de la danse. Lausanne: Édition Clairefontaine 1954. 134 p. Mo.

*GABATSHWANE, Sidwell Mhaladi. Botswana.

Tshekedi Khama of Bechuanaland, great statesman and politician. Cape Town: Oxford University Press 1961. X. 69 p. B.

[236]

*GATHERU, Reuel John Mugo. Kenya.

Child of two worlds. London: Routledge & Kegan Paul 1964. XIV, 215 p. ARo.

*GEOGRE, Crispin. Sierra Leone.

Precious gems unearthed by an African. Ilfracombe: Arthur H. Stockwell 1952. 63 p. Lyr.

GUMA, *Samson Mbizo*. South Africa.

\# Morena Mohlomi, mora Monyane. S. Sotho. Pietermartizburg: Shuter & Shooter 1960. 140 p. B.

HENSHAW, James Ene. Nigeria.

\# Medicine for love; a comedy. London: University of London Press 1964. 108 p. Th.

HUTCHINSON, Alfred. South Africa.

\# The rain-killers; a play. London: University of London Press 1964. 80 p. Th.

ad 891 do arab: Al-tarīq ilā Ghānā. Tr. Al-Sa'īd Muhammād Badawī. al-Qāhirah: Mu'assasat Sijill al-'arab 1964. 311 p. ANar.

ad 891 do rom: Drumul spre Ghana. Bucuresti: Editura politica 1964. 208 p. ANar.

*JABAVU, Davidson Don Tengo. South Africa.

E-America. Xhosa. Lovedale, South Africa: Lovedale Press 1932. 52 p. Itin.

E-Indiya. Xhosa. Lovedale, South Africa: Lovedale Press 1951. Itin.

E-Jerusalem. Xhosa. Lovedale, South Africa: Lovedale Institution Press 1928. VIII, 124 p. Itin.

The life of John Tengo Jabavu, editor of Imvo Zabantsundu, 1884-1921. Lovedale, South Africa: Lovedale Institution Press 1922. 154 p. B.

*JEBODA, Femi. Nigeria.

Olowolaiyemo. Yoruba. Ibadan, Nigeria: Longmans, Creen 1961. II, 142 p. ill. Nar.

*JOACHIM, Paulin. Dahomey.

Un nègre raconte. Paris: Éditions B. Durocher 1961. Lyr.

KAMITONDO, E. Ndopu. Zambia.

\# Ba ba lobalize lilumo mwa bulozi. Lozi. Cape Town: Oxford University Press 1960. VIII, 44 p. The mission histories series.

KHAKETLA, Bennett Makalo. Lesotho.
Dipjhamahte. S. Sotho. Johannesburg: Bona Press 1963.
IV, 86 p.
KHWELA, Simeon Thandindawo Zeblon. South Africa.
Simeon Thandindawo Zeblon Khwela & Otty Ezrom
Howard Nxumalo: Ukubhalwa kwezincwadi. Zulu. Pieter-
maritzburg: Shuter & Shooter 1961. 124 p. Nars.
*KITCHIN, Moabi S.
Boswa jwa puo . . .
vid. Lekgetho, J.M.
*KITCHIN, Neo H.
Boswa jwa puo . . .
vid. Lekgetho, J.M.
*KYERTWIE, K. O. Bonsu. Ghana.
Ashanti heroes. Accra, Ghana: Waterville 1964. VIII, 61 p.
Nars.
*LADIPO, Duro. Nigeria.
Three Yoruba plays: Oba koso, Oba moro, Oba waja. Eng-
lish adaptation by Ulli Beier. Ibadan, Nigeria: Mbari publi-
cations 1964. 75 p. Th.
*LARA, Ernesto Pires Barreto de, i.e., Ernesto Lara Filho,
Angola Picada de marimbondo; poemas. Nova Lisboa, An-
gola: Publicacões Bailundo 1961. 35 p. Coleccã Bailundo, 2.
Lyr.
*LEKEBA, S.P. Lesotho?
Gauta e Ntjhapile. S.Sotho. Johannesburg: Afrikaanse Pers-
Boekhandel 1961. 53 p. Nar.
*LEKGETHO, J.M. South Africa.
J.M. Lekgetho & Moabi S. Kitchin & Neo H. Kitchin:
Boswa jwa puo. Lobatse, Botswana: Bechuanaland Book
Centre 1961. 143 p. Dikwalo tsoo Tau. The Mackenzie
series, 1. Lyr.
*LEPHAKA, J. South Africa.
Ka ema-ema ka reta dibuta. Pedi. Johannesburg: Afrikaanse
Pers-Boekhandel 1961? 51 p. Lyr.
Konkong. Pedi. Johannesburg: Afrikaanse Pers-Boekhandel
1961? 35 p. Lyr.
* LEROTHOLI, George Basutoland.
Dithoko tsa mornea e moholo Seiiso Griffith. S.Sotho.
Morija: Morija Sesuto Book Depot 1940. 1962. 32 p. Lyr.

LESORO, Ephraim *Alfred Shadrack*. Lesotho?
\# Mmitsa. S.Sotho. Johannesburg: Afrikaanse Pers-Boekhandel
1961. IV, 28 p. Lyr.
\# Mathe-malodi. S. Sotho. Cape Town: Via Afrika 1964. XVII,
60 p.
\# Tau ya ha Zulu: tshwantshiso e ngotsweng ke. S.Sotho.
Johannesburg: Bona Press 1964. VIII, 60 p.
LUTHULI, Albert John. South Africa.
ad 937 do ned: Vrijheid voor mijn volk. Tr: Margrit de
Sablionière. Nijkerk: Callenback 1964. 288 p. A.
*MABOEE, Austin Teboho. South Africa.
Menyepetsi ya maswabi. S.Sotho. Johannesburg: Afrikaanse
Pers-Boekhandel 1963. 105 p. Ro.
*MACHAKA, Samson Rasebilu. South Africa.
Mahlodi ya polelo. . . Pedi. Johannesburg: Afrikaanse Pers-
Boekhandel 1962. 131 p. Lyr.
MADIBA, Moses Josiah Sekxwadi. South Africa.
⚌ Nkotsana. Pedi. Pretoria, South Africa: Van Schaik 1963.
72 p.
\# Tsiri. Pedi. Pretoria, South Africa: Van Schaik 1960. 38 p.
*MAKGALENG, Managase Macheng. South Africa.
Tswala e a ja. Pedi. Pretoria, South Africa: Van Schaik
1964. 45 p. Th.
MAKWALA, *Silpha Phaladi Ngwako*. South Africa.
\# Kgasane. Pedi. Pretoria, South Africa: Van Schaik 1962
47 p. Th.
MAMOGOBA, Phorohlo. South Africa.
\# Kgamphuphu. Pedi. Johannesburg: Afrikaanse Pers-Boek-
handel 196–. 84 p. Nars.
*MANYASE, Lenchman Thozamile. South Africa.
Imazi yezapholo. Xhosa. Cape Town: Via Afrika 1962. 26
p. Nar.
Umlu kaphalo; incwadi yezibongo samabanga apheZulu.
Zulu. Johannesburg: Bona Press 1960. 99 p. Lyr.
MATHIVHA, *Matshaya Edward Razwimisani*. South Africa.
\# Mabalanganye. Venda. Johannesburg: Afrikaanse Pers-
Boekhandel 1963. V, 86 p. Nars.
*MATLALA, Elias Koena Kgatishi. South Africa.
Mengwalô puku II. Pedi. Johannesburg: Goldfields Press
s.a. 61 p. E.

Tshukudu Pedi. Bloemfontein: Nasionale Pers-Boekhandel 1941. 92 p. Th. do: Pietermaritzburg: Mandate Investments 1958. 249 p. Th + Nars.

MATSEPE, Oliver Kgadime. South Africa.

\# Sebata-kgomo. Pedi. Johannesburg: Afrikaanse Pers-Boekhandel 1961. 83 p.

MENSAH, Toussaint Viderot. Togo.

\# Courage! Paris: Ed. Hautefeuille 1957. 93 p. Lyr.

*MILHEIROS, Mário. Angola.

Entre negros e corsários. Luanda, Angola: Edicões Mondego 1957. 215 p. Ro.

MOFOKENG, Sophonia Machabe. Lesotho?

\# Pelong ya ka. S.Sotho. Johannesburg: Witwatersrand University Press 1962. V, 95 p. Bantu treasury XV. E.

MOILOA, *James Jantjies.* Lesotho.

\# Dipale le metlae. S.Sotho. Cape Town: Via Afrika 1963. 116 p. Nars.

*MOJAKI, Philip J. South Africa.

Makolwane a kajeno; dithoko le dithothokiso. S.Sotho. Cape Town: Miller 1962. 62 p. Lyr.

MOPELI-PAULUS, Atwell Sidwell. Lesotho.

\# Moshweshwe moshwaila. S.Sotho. Johannesburg: Bona Press 1964. IV, 57 p.

MOROKE, Samson *Alexander.* Botswana.

\# Lehufa le lwa le thuto. Tswana. Cape Town: Via Afrika 1962. VI, 90 p.

\# Sephaphati. Tswana. Cape Town: Via Afrika 1959. V, 136 p.

MPASHI, Stephen Andrea. Zambia.

\# Abapatili bafika ku Babemba. Bemba. 2nd ed. Cape Town: Oxford University Press 1962. IV, 35 p. Mission histories series. Nar.

MPHAHLELE, Ezekiel. South Africa.

ad 1030 do sln: Druga avenija. Tr: Andrija Stancić. Novi Sad: Bratstvo-jedinstvo 1964. 336 p. A.

MQHAYI, Samuel Edward Krune. South Africa.

ad 1040 Ityala lamaWele; namanye a Mabali akwaXhosa. Xhosa. Complete ed. Lovedale, South Africa: Lovedale press 1961. 105 p. Ro.

\# U Bomi buka J.K. Bokwe. Xhosa. A biography of the

Rev. J.K. Bokwe. Lovedale, South Africa: Lovedale Press 193–. B.

Um Hlekazi uHintsa. Xhosa. Lovedale, South Africa: Lovedale Press 193–. Lyr.

MQHAYI, Samuel Edward Krune.

USeGqumahashe. Xhosa. A biography of the Chief N.C. Umhala. Lovedale, South Africa: Lovedale Press 193–. B.

*MULONGESA, Moses Chinyemba Bulaya. South Africa.
Vishimo vya kuuko. Luvale. Cape Town: Longmans, Green 1962. IV, 20 p. Nar.

MUTOMBO, Dieudonné Congo.

ad 647 Victoire de l'Amour. Leverville, Congo: Bibliothèque de l'Etoile 1957. Ro.

MUTSWAIRO, Solomon *Matsva*. Southern Rhodesia.

Feso. Shona. Cape Town: Oxford University Press in association with the Southern Rhodesia African Literature Bureau 1956. 84 p. ill. Nars.

Madetembedzo. . .
vid. Shamuyarira, M.

NDAWO, Henry Masila. South Africa.

ad 1063 U-Nolishwa. Xhosa. Lovedale, South Africa: Lovedale Press 1958. 123 p. Ro.

ad 1064 U-Nomathamsznqa noSigebenga. Xhosa. Lovedale, South Africa: Lovedale Press 1958. 60 p. Nar.

NTSANE, Kem Edward. Lesotho.

Nna sajene kokobela. S.Sotho. Johannesburg: Afrikaanse Pers-Boekhandel 1963. III, 105 p. Ro.

NWANKWO, Nkem. Nigeria.

Eroya; a play. Ibadan, Nigeria: University College, Ibadan, Dept. of Extra Mural Studies 1963. 23 p. Th.

ad 423 Tales out of school. illus. by Adebayo Ajayi. 1st ed. Lagos, Nigeria: African University Press 1963. 90 p. African reader's library 2. NarsKB.

NXUMALO, Otty Ezrom Howard *Mandla*. South Africa.

Ikusasa alaziwa. Zulu. Johannesburg: Bona Press 1964. VIII, 124 p.

Ukubhalwa kwezincwadi. . .
vid. Khwela, Simeon Thandindawo Zeblon.

NYABONGO, Akiki K. Uganda.

Hadithi za wabisoro. Swahili. Oxford: B. Blackwell 1937.

2 vols.—do abr. ed. Oxford: B. Blackwell 1937. 111 p. — do complete ed. Hadithi za wanyama. 2 vols. London: Sheldon Press 1961. Nars.

NYEMBEZI, Cyril Lincoln Sibusiso. South Africa.
\# A review of Zulu literature. Pietermaritzburg: University of Natal Press 1961. 10 p. E.

*ODEKU, E. Latunde. Nigeria.
Twilight out of the night. Ibadan, Nigeria: Aut. 1964. 139 p. Lyr.

ODOI, N.A. Ghana.
\# Facts to remember. Accra, Ghana: Presbyterian Book Depot 1961. 151 p. Nars.

ODUNJO, J.F. Nigeria.
\# Ọmọ òkú òrun. Yoruba. Lagos, Nigeria: African University Press 1964. 52 p. ill. RoKB

*OGUNDE, Hubert. Nigeria.
Yoruba ronu. Yaba, Nigeria: Pacific Printers 1964. Th.

OKOYE, Mokwugo. Nigeria.
\# African responses. Ilfracombe: Stockwell 1964. 420 p. Ro.

OLISAH, Sunday Okenwa. *pseud:* Strong Man of the Pen. Nigeria.
\# The life story and death of Mr. Lumumba. Onitsha, Nigeria: Aut. 1964. 55 p. B.

OLIVEIRA, Mário António Fernandes de. Angola.
\# Poesias. Lisboa: 1956. 16 p. Lyr.

OSÓRIO, Ernesto Cochat. Angola.
\# O homen do chapéu. Sá da Bandeira, Angola: Aut. 1962. 35 p. Nar.

OYONO, Ferdinand Léopold. Cameroun.
ad 524 do russ: Zizn' boja.   Tr: O. Moiseenko.
Moskva: Izd. hudoz. lit. 1964. 151 p. Ro.

* PETERS, Lenrie. Gambia.
Poems. Ibadan, Nigeria: Mbari Publications 1964: 44 p. Lyr.

*PIRES, Antonio. Angola.
Sangue Cuanhama; romance. Lisboa: Divisão de Publicacões e Biblioteca, Agência Geral das Colónias 1949. 176 p. Ro.

PLAATJE, Solomon Tshekisho. South Africa.
ad 1106 Mhudi; an epic of South African native life a hun-

dred years ago. 2nd ed. Lovedale, South Africa: Lovedale
Press 1957. 225 p. Ro.

*QABAKA, Mmeli Israel. South Africa.

Izanzulwana. Xhosa. Lovedale, South Africa: Lovedale
Press 1961. 145 p.

RABEARIVELO, Jean-Joseph. Malagasy.

Chants pour Abéone. Tananarive, Malagasy: Impr. Henri
Vidalie 1936. Lyr.

ad 710? Presque-songes, poemes Hova, traduits par l'auteur.
Tananarive, Malagasy: Impr. de l'Imerina 1934. Lyr.

Vieilles chansons des pays d'Imerina. Tananarive, Mala-
gasy: Impr. Officielle 1937. Lyr.

RABEMANANJARA, Jacques. Malagasy.

ad 716 Lamba. 2nd ed. Intr: Aimé Césaire. Paris: Présence
Africaine 1961. 84 p. Lyr.

*RAMAILA, M. Emma. South Africa.

Direto. Pedi. 2nd ed. Pretoria: Van Schaik 1961. 32 p. Lyr.

*RAMAILA, Ephafras Mogababise. South Africa.

Seriti sa Thabantsho: direto tsa magosi le bagale. Pedi.
Johannesburg: Afrikaanse Pers-Boekhandel 1959. 127 p. Lyr.

RIVE, Richard Moore. South Africa.

ad 1118 Emergency; a novel. London: Faber & Faber 1964. 251
p. Ro.

ROBERT, Shaaban. Tanganyika.

ad 740 Kusadikika nchi iliyo angani. Swahili. London: Nelson
1964. VI, 57 p. Nar.

ad 739 Maisha yangu. Swahili. Edinburgh: Nelson 1964. VIII,
67 p. Nars & Lyr.

ad 743 Pambo la Lugha. Swahili. Johannesburg: Witwatersrand University Press 1960. 49 p. Bantu treasury, 11. Lyr.

SADJI, Abdoulaye.

La belle histoire de Leuk-le-Lièvre . . .

vid. Senghor, Léopold Sédar.

SAKUBITA, M.M. Zambia.

Za luna li lu siile. Lozi. London: Macmillan 1954. do
Reprint with corrections 1958. VII, 39 p. Nar.

SAM, Gilbert A. Ghana.

A tragedy in Kumasi. Accra, Ghana: Gillisam Publishing
Syndicate 1960. 25 p. Kanzaar series, 24. Nar.

Seboni, Michael Ontepetse Martinus. Botswana.

\# Diane le maele a Setswana. Tswana. Lovedale, South Africa: Lovedale press 1962. 206 p. Ro.

\# Kgosi isang pilane. Tswana. Johannesburg: Afrikaanse Pers-Boekhandel 1961. 56 p. Nar.

Senghor, Léopold Sédar. Sénégal.

ad 553 Léopold Sédar Senghor & Abdoulaye Sadji: La belle histoire de Leuk-le-Lièvre; cours élémentaire des écoles d'Afrique noire. Illus. de Marcel Jeanjean. Paris: Hachette 1961. 173 p. ill. KB.

ad 564 [engl] Selected poems. Tr. & Intr: John Reed & Clive Wake. New York: Athenaeum 1964. XIX, 99 p. Lyr.

*Shamuyarira, M. Southern Rhodesia.

M. Shamuyarira & Matsva S. Mutswairo & B.M. Chivaura: Madetembedzo: Akare, akaunganidzwa. Shona. Cape Town: Longmans, Green in association with the Southern Rhodesia African Literature Bureau 1959. 32 p. Lyr.

Silveira, Onésimo. Cabo Verde.

\# Toda a gente fala: Sim, senhor. Sá da Bandeira, Angola: Publicacões Imbondeiro 1960 or 1961. 35 p. Coleccão Imbondeiro, 9. Lyr.

Sinxo, Guybon *Budlwana*. South Africa.

ad 1134 Imfene kadebeza neminye imidlalwana. Xhosa. Cape Town: Oxford University Press 1960. XIV, 105 p. Th.

\# Isakhono somfazi namanye amabalana. Xhosa Johannesburg: Afrikaanse Pers-Boekhandel 1958. 66 p. Nar.

\# Isitiya. Xhosa. Lovedale, South Africa: Lovedale Press 1964. 109 p. Nars.

Sithole, Ndabaningi. Southern Rhodesia.

ad 1141 do esp: El reto de Africa. Tr: Francisco González Aramburo. Mexico City: Fondo de Cultura Económica 1961. 228 p. ANar.

*Siwisa, L.K. South Africa.

Amabali angemigudu. Xhosa. Cape Town: Via Afrika 1962. V, 42 p. Nar.

Imidlalo yokulinganiswa. Xhosa. Pietermaritzburg: Shuter & Shooter 1963. 98 p.

Soromenho, Castro, Mocambique.

\# A aventura e a morte no sertão: Silva Pôrto e a viagem de

[244]

Angola a Mocambique. Lisboa: Livraria Clássica Editora 1943. 82 p. Coleccão Gládio, 11. Nar.

STEPHEN, Felix N. Nigeria.

How to make love. Onitsha, Nigeria: Njoku and sons, 1963. 48 p. Nar.

The trials and death of Lumumba. Onitsha, Nigeria: M. Allan Obejesi 1963. 44 p. Th.

STRONG MAN OF THE PEN, Pseud., *vid.* item No. 588 in Jahn's Bibliography, *vid.* Olisah, Sunday Okenwa.

SUTHERLAND, Efua Theodora. Ghana.

The roadmakers. Planned and written by E.Th. Sutherland. Photos. by W.E. Bell. Accra, Ghana: Ghana Information Service 1961. unpaged, Itin.

ad 589 do mold: Tu-ma-tu. Tr: A Blanovskij. Kisinev: Kartja moldovenjaske 1964. 51 p. ill. KB.

TCHICAYA U Tam'si, Gérald Félix. Congo.

Le ventre. Paris: Présence Africaine 1964. 135 p. Lyr.

VIDEROT MENSAH, Toussaint.

vid. Mensah, Toussaint Viderot.

*ZAMA, J. Mdelwa. South Africa.

Isinkwa sethu semihla ngemihla. Zulu. Pietermaritzburg: Shuter & Shooter 1960. VI, 96 p.

BIOGRAPHI-
CAL SKETCHES
OF AUTHORS

Biographical Sketches of Authors

I. CHOONARA. South African now living in London. Has had previous publication in *Transatlantic Review* and *The Christian.*

LAURA DAVIDSON. A graudate of the University of California, Berkeley, and a doctoral student in African literature at the University of Wisconsin at Madison.

DAVID DIOP. Killed in a plane crash en route from Paris to Dakar in 1960 at the age of thirty-three. See page 214.

JEAN IKELLE-MATIBA. Novelist born in Cameroun, residing in West Germany. See page 211.

ELLEN CONROY KENNEDY. Mrs. Kennedy, who has contributed articles and reviews on French-speaking African writers to *Africa Report, African Forum,* and *Negro Digest,* has translated *Lyrical and Critical Essays* by Albert Camus, edited by Phillip Thody.

[249]

LEONARD KIBERA. Kenyan playwright and short-story writer. Mr. Kibera won third prize at the BBC African Drama Contest in 1967 with *The Potent Ash* published here. He is co-author of a collection of short stories, *The Potent Ash,* together with Samuel Kahiga.

ROBERT E. MCDOWELL. Wrote his Ph.D. dissertation at the University of Denver on "African-English Novels." He is currently Assistant Professor of English at the University of Texas, Arlington, and a reviewer of Africana for *The Denver Post.*

ALIRWANA MUGALULA MUKIIBI. See page 218.

JOSEPH OKPAKU. Playwright-critic and editor of this volume. Mr. Okpaku is president and publisher of The Third Press in New York and Associate Professor at Sarah Lawrence College.

PAUL PÁRICSY. A Fellow of the Institute of the Hungarian Academy of Sciences, Vácrátót, Hungary.

OBIAGELI PETERS. A graduate of the University of Nigeria, Nsukka, and University of California, Los Angeles.

COSMO PIETERSE. A South African living in London, is editing a series of anthologies of African plays for Heinemann Educational Books.

ELINOR SCHIFFRIN. Cambridge, Massachusetts.

NANCY SCHMIDT. Anthropologist, Stanislaus State College, California. She holds a Ph.D. from Northwestern University.

PETER WANI SONGA. A graduate of University College, Dar Es Salaam.

PAULETTE J. TROUT. Holds a Ph.D. from Columbia University, has taught at Yale, Columbia, Barnard College, and U.C.L.A. She has published several articles on African literature in *Africa Report*.

GENE ULANSKY. Taught English and humanities for two years at the University of Nigeria, Enugu. At present he teaches English at Golden Gate College, San Francisco.

DONALD J. WEINSTOCK. Lecturer in English at the University of California, Riverside.

DATE DUE

Dec 8 '71 W			
76 AC			
Jun 9 78 S			
0 0 Jun20 78			
JUN 2 '90 S			
GAYLORD			PRINTED IN U.S.A.